Heaven on Earth

TALA SCOTT

BALBOA
PRESS

A DIVISION OF HAY HOUSE

Balboa Press books may be ordered through booksellers or by contacting:

Balboa Press
A Division of Hay House
1663 Liberty Drive
Bloomington, IN 47403
www.balboapress.com.au
1 (877) 407-4847

Printed in the United States of America.

ISBN: 978-1-4525-2415-3 (sc)
ISBN: 978-1-4525-2416-0 (e)

Balboa Press rev. date: 07/30/2014

Dedication

To my beautiful children
Thank you for your loving support

My heart-felt thanks to my soul family
And to those who believe in love

Contents

Author's Note

Heaven on Earth is a true story written to convey an important message. The message reveals the sacred teachings of a relationship that is destined to heal the family and spark an evolutionary process. The decision to share my family's private details was not taken lightly. We have journeyed along the life path from fear to love allowing time to heal our emotional wounds. This healing has enabled my family to experience the blessing of peace and harmony. People's names have been changed to protect their privacy. I honour the contribution they have given me toward the teaching of experiential learning. If just one person's life is enhanced or healed then we have achieved what we set out to do. Our life purpose is to assist others as they awaken to discover the glory of an incredible life.

Preface

Heaven on Earth. Three simple words. These three simple words will change our world and the way we perceive our relationships. Heaven on Earth is a true story; revealing a sacred relationship that links us at the level of the heart, body, soul and mind. Its activation lays dormant, hidden in the deepest recess of the heart; a gateway to an incredible new world.

As we view our world today, we see that it does not reflect a peaceful, loving environment. It is filled with fear, inequality, pain and violence as we strive to obtain answers concerning our current dilemmas. World peace cannot be found in solutions that exist outside of us. Love, peace, tolerance and compassion can only be known and acknowledged first from within.

The heart field contains a key that allows us to explore the balance between ancient wisdom and new information. This information will reveal the path to find a resonance that can link our differences, combine our strengths and project compassion to the world as we learn to embrace higher truths first hand.

My only objective is to show you a new way to love, a new way to live and a new way to experience a world of peace and joy far removed from the pain and suffering many people experience today.

Revealed in the jewel of this story is a concept your heart lovingly knows, but for now, has temporarily forgotten. It is time to remember, to awaken from the illusions of life and take responsibility in finding the miracles that are rightfully ours.

Introduction

Within the heart of the world family resides the loving embrace of our own. My immediate family consists of my adored children Luca, Marc, Bella and Lorenzo. I know that I am truly blessed to share my life with them. Their love filters through my heart and the flow is unconditional.

I have been entrusted to share with you detailed experiences of my life's journey. As you embark upon this journey, I invite you to step into the new frontier of a relationship called Divine Union. It is here we discover secrets; a doorway to an incredible new life.

My first of many dream visions occurred when I was three years old. A childhood accident opened the portal to the realm of dream vision experiences. As time evolved they became prophetic; a glimpse beyond our everyday reality. I would close my eyes searching for the slumbering surrender of sleep only to awaken to conscious thoughts again. During the process of dreaming, I access my Higher Self and experience real life events. Upon waking, an indescribable feeling of love and joy resides deep within my heart. As I grew in age and maturity the adult visions foretold the importance of Divine Union. They also explored the sacredness of sexuality, providing information to be utilised for teaching at a later time.

As time evolved it became abundantly clear that I needed to transcribe what I had learnt, to share my work via the written word. A book? Initially the idea was too overwhelming for me to consider. For many years I tried to convince my friends and colleagues of their authenticity to complete the work that had been asked of me. In times of doubt I placated my rational mind, convincing myself that I knew very little concerning such matters. Information of this importance would need documentation, verification and a university degree at least. I would learn much later that this would not be necessary for I had graduated with Honours from the University of Life Education.

Higher education did evade my life path, however, the literary world initially beckoned during childhood. I reveal a reverence of truth; I genuinely love to read. My mother would find me curled in my bed, the glow of a wispy candle the only sustaining beacon of light. Of course she would be furious at my obvious attempts to thwart her disciplinary action. The lights were turned off at seven-thirty: much too early for my enquiring mind. I accepted her attempt to mould me as necessary but also futile. A higher loving presence has always guided my heart and mind.

During my late-night sojourns I would read books where characters, places and events became real in my conscious world and I would be transported to a place of mystique, the original source the author uses to create. I once believed this magical place could be tapped into at will. Now, armed with a little more experience, I know for certain this is our higher connection of love.

The writing of Heaven on Earth is my life purpose. The information it contains is clear and concise, encased in words of sheer simplicity. Concepts of simplicity are familiar to me. I am aware, however, that sometimes these concepts are the most difficult of all to comprehend. Does not our most profound pearl of wisdom anchor around the timeless truth that we are born to love one another? Simplicity itself, yet this is impossible for us to achieve on a global level as yet.

During our lives we hurt each other, intentionally and unintentionally. Feelings of hurt and disappointment are created as we shut our heart to the truth of the ancient wisdom known as divine love. Now is the time to heal our emotional wounds. This will allow cohesion to flow in our lives and will encourage us to find a way to express true love as we actively participate in the process of life.

You will be shown first-hand the euphoria of the love I have found. This love is wordless in wisdom, demanding in honesty, pure in content and it lives eternally in your soul. The access lays dormant, just out of reach until you are ready to locate the key.

My own healing has been a journey of recovery and discovery. Each level of healing produced new and amazing insights. I invite you once more to step into the new frontier of the heart, body, soul and mind. If you choose to do so, I promise you implicitly that your life will never be the same. You will be asked to trust in a power more amazing than anything you could hope to wish for; an unspoken promise of a dream that will manifest as truth.

As you read these pages an amazing story will unfold. Its reason for being is to inspire, uplift and teach humanity a new way to love, and in expressing this love, a new way to live. Its purpose is to create amazing differences in the lives of all who are touched by it.

The First Glimpse

I have never been a material girl. The thought of diamonds parading in their own splendour has never captured the attention of my heart. The diamond essence to capture my heart is whispered in the eternal flow of our stars, a gateway to incredible worlds beyond. Their essence is engaged in a secret knowing, lovingly cradled within the soft embrace of our universe. Our universe is awe-inspiring with its ebb and flow, exuding the soft tenderness of the mother and the humble strength of the father.

Within my heart is a story I have been entrusted to share with you, a story yet the truth of a sacred love destined to change the way we think forever.

I am woken in a dream vision with the remembrance of surreal surroundings. I find myself lying across my ebony wrought-iron bed. White silk curtains are billowing to the caress of a gentle breeze. A man appears in front of me smiling, assuming that I will recognise him. He is very confident and assured with his unique level of understanding. I return his smile while trying to conceal the exquisite sensation I feel in my body. I move my gaze and find to my delight that he is standing before me in his birthday suit and yes,

1

he has forgotten to attach his fig-leaf! His smile, glowing with the freedom of child-like innocence plays around his soft sensuous lips.

My heart sways to the beat of his energy rhythm, confirming a replica image of my own. His handsome face reveals eyes that mirror my soul, sparkling brown eyes that shine anew with the essence of liquid honey. He is touching me with his eyes, accessing my sacred place within. An intense heat reverberates around my arms, shoulders, neck and head causing me to feel light-headed, yet intensely aware of his magnetic presence.

He raises one eyebrow and says, "Take my hand; I have something to show you."

My smile reveals the tantalising delight of the chemistry that is transpiring between us. For now, however, he is intently focused on a special project. I place my hand in the contours of his and our cells dance to the beat of a familiar drum. Physical sensation claims my attention and I realise that we are moving.

Our bodies are slowly drawn together as we move into a spiralling vortex of light. The combined energy creates a pattern of golden light. We are bathed in this light, the sensation of pure love is emanating from within. My mind is busy comprehending the fact that we are no longer touching the ground. Instinctively I move my head and look incredulously into a myriad of stars. The most amazing sound echoes drowning my normal senses beneath the sea of no mind. Within my cells converges the same inner experience. The convergence of harmony, a sliver of pure divine love pulsates as energy vibrates all around me, allowing us to feel Oneness.

Reaching toward the stars I am aware of an intense whoosh of energy. Words defy description as I acknowledge that I am playing with my beloved stars. Their energy pulsates within me, and my energy reverberates within them. Divine love is the intricate linking thread. My eyes shimmer with the dust of silver tears, I am speechless. This beautiful man has accessed the path to my heart's desire and manifested a promise he made long ago. The chamber of my heart flutters like the dance of butterfly wings.

A beautiful hand is placed gently on my waist. I instinctively move toward him, close enough to know that my body would fit perfectly with his. A knowing abounds that we could merge and become One. An unimaginable joy bubbles its way into my conscious reality and I know this moment will be imprinted on my heart for a lifetime.

Two soulful brown eyes look adoringly into my own. His energy pulsates, flaming into a fiery life-force of its own. The full moon glows. Her light shimmers like gossamer wings, she winks, acknowledging her approval. His slender fingers hold the back of my head; the sensation captures feelings that are divine. His eyes shine portraying unconditional love—Christ-like in purity and intent.

A chain of golden light encircles my heart pulling me closer toward him. His lips glide effortlessly across my bottom lip. They are gentle, yet demanding my full attention. Glorious sensation cascades over my over-active cells. He repeats this pleasure with my top lip, purposefully thorough in the joy of his discovery. His hands cup my face while his thumbs caress my skin with a passion that needs to be known. Tenderly his lips open to claim mine. I shiver involuntarily. He tastes of nectar. The ancients refer to this nectar as the sacred divine. My Spirit—the real inner me jumps out of the safety of my physical body into the sanctuary of his waiting arms. The force of the contact creates vibrating surges of bliss. Radiating around his body is a golden glow. It sparkles with flickering particles encased by intertwining tubes of light. His hands slide down my back, gently guiding my body closer to him. His kiss deepens; his soul's love wraps itself protectively around my heart. Our bodies, now connected begin to vibrate. The vibration is gentle at first. Within a few minutes it ripples in intensity from the tops of our heads to the tips of our toes. We are merging—heart, body, soul and mind. My body isn't registering any feeling, just an all-encompassing love beyond limit that is pureness itself. At this point I wonder if my physical atoms are going to explode or die. Sensing my reaction his kiss softens and slows in intensity. Reluctantly, it is time to return. His beautiful hand holds mine, reassuring me that when he is with me I am always safe and protected. As light as a feathered wing, we descend into the reality of everyday life.

I awoke to the feeling of sheer delight. Golden sun-rays were beaming on the right-hand side of the window reminding me that I was very much alive and well. I opened one eye and peeked beneath my doona just to make sure I was still occupying my body. Oh, what blessed relief! My children would be really upset if I had ascended and evaporated in a puff of smoke!

My lips tingled. The memory of my dream vision was crystal clear. I grinned. Sparkling eyes, cheeky smiles and surreal confidence were soon to become a permanent part of my nature. The vision offered me an opportunity to learn so much regarding the concept of Divine Union. It was beyond my simple understanding about love. I held a deep mistrust in my heart concerning men. My past experiences had not been kind. However, thoughts of intrigue lingered. Sighing deeply, I concluded that it was time to embrace the day.

As I drove to work a few hours later, I replayed the dream vision in my mind. Intuitively, I knew the encounter was sacred. For a few precious moments we had been given the key to Divine Union. We had been given the first glimpse. A miracle evolved effortlessly, waiting to unfold in a future time. Disregarding my readiness to accept miracles unfolding around me, Heaven on Earth was a happening thing!

The Journey of Love

My dream vision had now stirred my heart and changed my life forever. Divine Union allows us to experience true love—the most powerful love we can know. This love provides us with the opportunity to live an incredibly fulfilling life as we explore and discover miracles. Divine love will stir your life as an awakening. It may start as a whisper pressed softly against your ear. It may start as an explosion of pure bliss in your heart. Life is a path of adventure expressing many memorable moments—the greatest highs and the lowest lows. The path in between opens the gate to the entry of life lessons. The only requirement you need is an open heart and mind.

Each one of us is born unique but connected to family through cellular memory. My family life has taught me the lesson of unconditional love. To enhance my life purpose, I have chosen to give birth to four children. In my sane, rational moments, I believe my choice reveals great wisdom. In my insane, irrational moments I questioned my choice and the degree of my sanity.

My eldest child, my son Luca, is now thirty. After his birth, I reflected in the still moment of recovery and I remember the feeling of awe knowing that I had given birth to our child. The grandeur of this feeling was to be replaced with absolute panic as I realised that we would be responsible for shaping and guiding his life for the next twenty-one years. His dark blue eyes gazed at mine; searching for our soul connection and these words his soul knew.

"I am your first-born child and through me you will learn all of your first parenting mistakes. I will produce Oscar winning tantrums in shopping centres. I will not speak until I am three years old because I choose not to. At thirteen I will have my first alcoholic drink because I will love to shock you. I will spend hours discussing life's intricate flow and of course girls! During my school years I will express my concern to my Catholic schoolteachers as I explain that God lives in the heart, not in the dogma of outdated rules that squash my soul. My peers will allow me to lead as we bond through the love of music. You will stand by my side, always loving me, believing in my true heart. I will leave my lessons behind to follow the spiritual path set before me, only to discover your footprints in the sand. I will teach and you will learn. You will teach and I will learn to honour the purity of your heart as we journey this life together."

My second child is also a son. Marc is now twenty-eight. Marc arrived into this world with very little fuss. As he rested with his tiny hand across my shoulder, his soft sweet face nuzzled against mine, his deep blue eyes held my gaze and these words his soul knew.

"I am your second child and I will wrap my tiny fingers around your heart. Our family connection will be deeply etched. I will break my bones; my thumb, wrist and arm before I am twelve years old. I will approach life like a bull in a china shop. Soccer will be my passion as I have a destiny to fulfil. My face radiates the cheekiest grin as I sing in the school choir. I will teach you that flatulence is not a dirty word, but a bodily function with musical attributes you would never dream of understanding. Five hundred people will witness my soccer success as I am honoured by my peers. You smile gently, acknowledging my humble heart while knowing the opportunity will take me further steps from you. In time I will leave you to honour my destiny but always your heart will walk hand-in-hand with mine. I will teach and you will learn. You will teach and I will make you laugh as we journey this life together."

My third child is a daughter. Bella is twenty-six. Her arrival into this world was pain-relief free. I fully expected another son so my shock was paramount as her umbilical cord was lifted and her arrival duly announced. It took three days for me to believe that this pink-clothed, dark-haired chocolate-eyed beauty was indeed mine. She lay peacefully across my legs with eyes of liquid pools that searched my face and these words her soul knew.

"I am the child born to heal the hurt in your heart. The true bond of mother and daughter will now be rectified and your dream will manifest. I will sing pop songs and know all the words when I am three years old. I will let you dress me in dresses of outrageous frills and lace. The door to puberty will open and I will ease through gently knowing that by then you will be really tired from raising my two brothers. My bedroom will be filled with awards for academic achievement, purity of heart, good manners and deep compassion for all. Our love will deepen as you allow me the freedom to stretch my wings as I travel from puberty to adulthood. I will watch as your heart opens, always encouraging me to love you more. You will teach and I will learn. I will teach and you will smile as we journey this life together."

My fourth child is another son. Lorenzo is twenty. Lorenzo is the child conceived in the initiation of my Divine Union awakening. His arrival into this world was painful physically and emotionally, with much pain and many stitches involved. Our love is deep, enduring the twists and turns of life's traversed road. His beautiful pale-blue eyes peeked from beneath his snow-white hat and these words his soul knew.

"I am the child conceived in pure love of Divine Union. I will encourage your sense of humour and teach you to stay young at heart. I will walk when I am nine months old and talk at eighteen months old. I will speak profound words of wisdom and then continue to play with my toy cars. Testing your unconditional love, I will stretch life's boundaries. You will treat me with love and respect, and mostly with patience knowing that I have life lessons to learn independently. My sense of humour will be my saving grace and yours many times. I will teach you to learn to dream that all things are possible. You will sigh as you say, "I will think about it," which means you have no intention of granting my unreasonable request as we journey this life together."

I have discovered in the ordinary of everyday life that we are capable of discovering and accessing the extraordinary. My lesson of unconditional love has accentuated my growth in so many profound ways. As I watched my children grow from babies to the fine adults they are today, a greater understanding of my own childhood lessons evolved.

Humble Beginnings

I was born on the 15ᵗʰ October 1960. My parents James and Olivia welcomed my arrival with joy. I am their eldest child. Six daughters were born in succession and then finally a son. Olivia was born deaf and mute. My maternal grandmother Joy contracted German measles in her first trimester. Olivia was educated at a school that specialised in teaching the blind and deaf. This linked her to the outside world. James was a musician with an insatiable love for jazz. He would frequent jazz clubs, and immerse himself in the music that provided nourishment for his soul. His parents Herbert and Margaret migrated from England during their early married life.

My great aunt Deanna, Joy's sister, was the matriarch of our family. Her heart held the capacity for great love. She cared for her children and so many other children who came into her home. When I was three months old, Olivia developed tuberculosis and had her left lung removed. Her recovery time was slow and tedious and within twelve months I was living permanently with Deanna. Home is where the heart is and to my parents I would never return. Destiny had provided for me a more expansive plan of karmic resolution, residing in the warm cocoon of unconditional love.

Deanna birthed eleven children, and as a baby I was provided with loving care and attention. As a child I was intrigued with learning and acquired basic reading and writing skills before attending school. I would sit for hours drawing lines on paper, convinced that I was writing books from a deep imaginary source. After a period of time I would gather family members together and ask them to read my stories out loud. Of course they couldn't. I hadn't formulated any words yet. They humoured me with gentleness and appreciation. Little by little they would make up stories, following my lead and a tale of some imaginable story would emerge and I would be applauded for my brilliant work.

My first glimpse into visionary worlds occurred when I was three. While playing a game of chasings with my cousins, I ran through the back garden and hit my forehead on a steel clothes-line pole. The force of the blow pushed me backward so hard that I hit the back of my head on a concrete path. Ouch! The bump on my head was painful and extremely tender to touch. It took a few weeks to heal.

A few months later my cousins came to visit. Once again we were gathered in the back garden, standing in a circle, holding hands. We were singing with great gusto, "We all fall down." I remember falling onto my back laughing with glee. As my head turned to the side the veil between worlds parted, and a rush of energy took my breath away momentarily. What I saw next will be imprinted on my heart forever.

Wispy mist covered the setting momentarily as I found my bearings. Through the veil I could see that we were holding hands standing on a cobbled street in France. Our designer clothes were made of expensive cloth and our shoes were soft, black leather. I was wearing dainty pointy-toe boots with a distinctive small sculptured heel. The streets were cobbled and as I looked to the side I could see slightly dilapidated stone buildings curving to the right. To the left were cafes, and the aroma of coffee and the delicious smell of baked pastries was so inviting. The scene disappeared after a few minutes, but the experience is still so fresh in my heart and mind today. I knew these children, we had lived before. Time and space connected as I glimpsed the loop of lifetimes merging into the ever-present now.

As I grew in age the visions became prophetic. I would keep the details of my visions to myself, telling no one. By the age of seven I could move around, exploring different dimensions, often losing precious minutes of time. I would return from my explorations with complete feelings of love and purity circling within and around my heart. Acceptance of my differences took many years to evolve. My childhood left a visible imprint of pain that surfaced from adolescence to adulthood. When I slipped into my visions, I was unable to hear anyone around me. A hearing test confirmed that my problem was not a medical condition. The diagnosis was childhood defiance and I was sent home accordingly.

Sometimes the feeling of infinite loneliness would threaten to seep down upon me like waves engulfing my thoughts and emotions. Dark pools of emotional strain laid claim to the prize of my sanity. My family sustained my physical needs, yet I continually struggled with my differences. Years would unfold in the tenuous touch of time before I would find the peace that evaded me, not knowing that a higher love was guiding my life to the destiny that lay in wait. Lessons, however, wait for no one.

My first life lesson was introduced when I was six years old. Olivia was having difficulty with her third pregnancy so my sister Charlotte was invited to stay with us. Sharing? Deanna was ecstatic. I was scared. Personally, I would have preferred to look after a soft cuddly teddy bear. My green-eyed jealousy monster reared its ugly head. On reflection, I realised that all I needed to hear Deanna say was that she still loved me, and that I was not going to be replaced by my sister. The words, however, remained unspoken.

I endured many years of guilt knowing the pain I inflicted on my sister. She was frightened and alone. The family she knew had been abruptly taken from her, leaving me as her only real connection to emotional stability. As a result of my insecurity, I would pinch Charlotte or pull her hair whenever she annoyed me, which was all of the time. She endured the pain in silence hoping that I would treat her with gentleness and kindness. Mostly, I felt like an outsider, watching the scene unfold from the outside looking in. Charlotte was allowed to share my friends, share my clothes and share my bed. As a final act of betrayal Deanna enrolled her at my primary school. When I was approached with this pearl of wisdom I outwardly smiled, but inwardly screamed no! Too late! It was decided and my freedom was finally clipped.

What I failed to see as a child, I realised as truth when I reached adulthood. Sometimes we share a closer bond with some family members than others. It is not a greater love but the outcomes of lessons still to be learnt. The lessons are to be sifted through until we can let go of the hurt and pain. Honestly, I was loved no less. I was loved deeply; the love remained unexpressed most of the time which only added to the frustration and pain-filled confusion of my precious child's heart. As early as six years of age I knew that we needed to resolve the problems we faced as a family. Why was no one listening?

Gradually life returned to normal and I was promoted to grade two the following year. My sister stayed behind in grade one. In tentative stages I opened my heart to my sister and learnt to trust and welcome the generosity of her heart. Olivia allowed Charlotte to stay with me, allowing Deanna to raise her too. This is the greatest gift she could have given me. Our closeness has endured the ebb and flow of life, enabling us to form a treasured bond of friendship that we still enjoy today.

Our home was a place of comfort. It was a common occurrence for relatives and friends to stay with us. During the festive time of Christmas holiday celebrations in 1969 we were introduced to a lady referred to as Nana. Nana was a lady who oozed finesse. She was the relative of a distant cousin so we adopted her as our own. Sitting around an open fire Nana explained that she was an orator and that her gift was passed down from her ancestors of tribal traditions. She recounted our family history.

I was born in a beautiful part of the world, an island paradise that is surrounded by the majesty of crystal blue waters. My great, great grandparents Walter and Sarah lived in a farming district well-known for its export of apples. The township is built on the foundation of community love. Walter was a hardworking handsome man, determined to leave a legacy for his family. His occupations were ship builder, land owner and inventor. He built the first apple-grader which saved manual time for his farm labourers. His greatest passion flowed around the love he felt for the land, a passion that swirls within our blood. During his lifetime Walter amassed large portions of land and passed away leaving considerable wealth for the generations of his bloodline to follow.

Or so he thought! Walter and Sarah produced one son and six daughters. Their son Charles was lazy, and having acquired drinking and gambling addictions he fritted away his inheritance forcing his wife and children to move to the capital city. Their beautiful home, filled with antique furniture and showcase cabinets of fine bone china was gone. All that remained were the memories and consideration of a humble man's pure intent. The consequences of the lessons to be learnt and the legacy of loss were handed down to the generations who followed.

Deanna was gifted with the voice of an angel. In her early twenties she was invited to travel to England to receive singing tuition. This opportunity would have created an amazing new life for her but Charles refused to let her go. Smothered by guilt and the disappointment of his own shortcomings he deemed that Deanna was indispensable to her family and she was forced to stay at home.

At this point in the story I could feel tears plopping onto my blue cotton dress. I was torn between feelings of sorrow toward Deanna and my selfish relief that she was still here mothering me. She had kept a secret deep inside her heart. Deanna wasn't allowed to attend school; she had not acquired formal education. Her father deemed it unnecessary. I was aware that this secret caused her intense pain. To fill her days Deanna was ordered to chop two tonne of wood each day in addition to helping her mother with daily chores.

During my life I would often hear Deanna question her father's motives in regard to his attitude toward her, and then in the same breath she would affirm that her life purpose was to assist everyone who found their way into her care. Sometimes I would feel the guilt surface and then Deanna would look into my eyes, connect with my real inner self, and the guilt would slide past me as if it was never really there. She always instilled in us the importance of telling the truth and we learnt very quickly that the truth was expected in return.

In many ways Deanna's innocence swirled within my soul. Her inability to communicate effectively with the world had a massive impact on her life, and as the future unfolded it would impact my life too. My greatest lesson of frustration arose when her inability to cope with the "real world" surfaced. If she was faced with any reasoning that was contrary to her belief system, it would send her into a rage. I would learn as an adult that her reaction was one of ignorance, not intentional on her part. She misunderstood many concepts that were common to others. In her wisdom she decided that my school days were the best days of my life. Try telling that to most adolescent girls!

Deanna's early life lessons cultivated great inner strength. I am convinced that her strength surfaced because she was faced with only two possibilities. Become strong or die. I would learn the latter was not in her vocabulary. Without formal education she deemed it her divine right to change the rules of life as it progressed. It only became confusing when I wasn't paying attention and the rules of the game changed.

In my young tender years I was savvy enough to understand that the changing rules of life might be a family tradition so I refocused my attention on Nana. As I watched her telling our family history I noticed that she exuded first-hand the magic of anticipation that was woven into her storytelling. She was showing me through sheer simplicity how easy this was to do.

The Beat Moves On

The memories of childhood and the frustrations I endured have now been replaced with love, understanding and acceptance. Compared to the fast pace of life today where we are able to reach the world via the internet, our family was encased in innocence and surrounded by the gentle country pace of our ancestors.

We shared weekends with our uncles, aunts and cousins. When personalities are immersed in a mix of so many temperaments there is much to learn. If I had chosen to pursue a career in psychology my relatives would have expanded my knowledge and understanding of the human mind and emotions tenfold. However, the varying degrees of love, patience, tolerance, acceptance and the ability to be non-judgemental come to the fore in my mind's eye.

Deanna's favourite sister Ruth married her childhood sweetheart and returned to the place of her birth and settled in her home town. The love between the sisters was evident to everyone. As a gift Ruth would spend many hours sewing chequered cotton underwear for all the girls. She presented them to us with much pride.

I remember looking at this very unattractive underwear thinking it must be a lampshade. How would I know? I was only five years old. I promise you, the size and density of these things were bloomers with wings. My femininity felt very threatened. I was horrified when it was explained to me that I was expected to wear them, but I did wear them for I knew that I had no choice. Freedom of speech and the opportunity to question or offer an opinion was left to the exploration of adults having earned the right. Twenty-one was this magical age. It seemed so far away. Childhood was the putty stage; a time of moulding, shaping and imagining, and learning to be seen and not heard. There was an upside to it though, and love was the bounteous treasure, oodles of love in every shape, depth and colour, and the exploring of the purity that was always crystal clear.

Friday and Saturday nights were times of the weekend retreats that my cousins looked forward to with relish. The adults would retire to the lounge room to discuss topics of importance, leaving us children alone to amuse ourselves. My male cousins would convince the girls to play in the barn. They would tell ghost stories, each tale more horrendous than the last, until exhaustion claimed my attention and I would fall asleep.

With a start I would be woken by howling that emerged from the dark unknown. I would scream, running to the exit only to find it locked. My screams would become blood curdling, escalating in volume until an adult would hear me and come to my rescue. My cousins would roll on the ground howling with fits of giggles followed by the feigned apologies hidden behind tenuous smirks and the inevitable promise not to frighten me again. I would accept their apology while sensing that it would only be a matter of time before the desire to torment me surfaced again.

During the weekend we spent time exploring every nook and cranny of the farm property. We built cubby houses, played in doll's houses, climbed trees, ate fruit and raw vegetables, collected eggs and talked to the chickens fussing in their coops. We marvelled at their yellow fluffy babies, mesmerised by the softness of their silky bodies. The smell of freshly baked bread, cakes and cookies laden on trays in the large family kitchen where the brightest light encircled the large wooden table, created memories that are still so fresh and clear in my mind today.

When the inevitable disagreement erupted each child would be herded like cattle and we were privy to view a court of law in session. Evidence was presented, the offending parties were talked to and Judge Deanna was in session waiting to deliver her verdict. We all knew what the outcome would be. If you were present, or involved in the disagreement in any way then you were found guilty. Guilty parties were given a tap on the backside with a wooden spoon. This was enough to stop us quickly in our tracks. Then peace would prevail and harmony would return like the gentle whisper of a soothing summer afternoon breeze.

After the hustle and bustle of the evening meal I would retire to my room and lie between the covers of my blankets and top sheet ready to devour my books. They provided me with first-hand knowledge about the outside world. It would be many, many years before I would directly experience the world. Reading books allowed me to become aware of how others lived and explored our glorious planet earth. This time of deep reflection, a reprieve from the deafening roar of chattering voices was also a time to access my visions, as at this stage I assumed that everyone could zip around the world in twenty minutes.

Christmas celebrations enabled us to explore the reverence of family life. Yet I was still an outsider looking in, unable to really connect with anyone. Santa delivered a swing set, a cubby house and a swimming pool into our back yard. Down the chimney he deposited clothes, a doll and various small toys. Christmas Eve was a time of magical interlude as we talked, deliberating for hours. Excitement would threaten to overwhelm and consume us until finally sleep arrived to transport us to the dreaming realms of sleep.

Christmas morning would finally arrive. We would sit on our beds until boredom set in. Our giggles would increase in volume and intensity until we heard Deanna's shrill voice reminding us that Santa might have changed his mind and not visited us at all. This horrific image quickly quietened us down. We were asked to wait another half an hour and then finally we were allowed to leave our rooms.

The lounge room was a sight to behold. The Christmas tree was adorned with ornaments and sparkling lights and each child was designated a specific area. As an adult I was awed and puzzled that Deanna could afford the items for nine children that were still living at home. They were all so beautifully displayed. The looks of true wonder, magic and delight were the only reward sought for the hours she spent cooking, cleaning and preparing that accompanied the responsibilities of being a widowed parent.

Older family members would arrive with their spouses and children for lunch and dinner respectively. Lunch consisted of meat, roast vegetables, fruit and ice-cream. Dinner was buffet style providing meats, fish, chicken, salads and dessert. We were also given a special treat of Christmas pudding in which was hidden five cent coins wrapped in foil. Unbeknown to us, each child was given equal amounts of coins to be spent a week later to purchase lollies.

The day was long, but exciting as we played backyard cricket and bowls. As evening approached, family members would return to their homes and I would watch Deanna breathe a sigh of relief and sit down for the first time. She was happy and content that she had served her family once again. We possessed little knowledge concerning the true material trappings of Christmas day. This day held for us the values of love, accepting family members into our home with their varying degrees of behaviour, singing carols around the piano and the splendour of wondering what it would be like to celebrate a white Christmas in England.

Christmas celebrations also evoke in the heart and mind memories of our loved ones who are no longer with us. Deanna's husband Tom was loved by her in the tradition of men and women of their generation in the early 1900s. Till death do we part! Her pain, her suffering and betrayal was endured in silence. Deanna's pain and frustration kept me protected and suffocated as she emotionally wrapped me in layers of cotton wool.

Tom died when I was twelve months old. He was adamant that I was meant to be part of their very large family and Deanna was equally committed and wanted to honour his last wishes. World War Two claimed four years of Tom's life. He was captured and tortured as a prisoner of war. His injuries and experiences were horrific, his inner turmoil other people could not understand. He remained in the army until a heart attack claimed his life in 1961.

With Tom's early return to his heavenly abode, our family became involved with a community group. They helped to nurture the children aged from seven to eighteen, giving them emotional care and nurture as a sign of respect. I was involved with sport, craft and drama. I loved it!

My first introduction to Deanna's broody overprotective nature occurred when I was ten years old. A community member visited my mother and requested her permission to submit a story I had written to a writer's competition. Deanna refused, offering no explanation. Was history repeating itself?

During the same year my grade four class was chosen as the inaugural group to be taught French. I was delighted. I displayed a perfect French accent, acquiring skill in the language as a kindred soul. My test results during primary and secondary school averaged ninety-eight per cent in accuracy.

A television station decided to film a documentary about primary school children who were participating in the language programme. Their objective was to showcase the children's progress. I was asked to participate. Fearing my mother's reaction I explained to her that I was participating in a school project. The film crew arrived and small butterflies started to circle in my tummy. I was given a script to read that I had learnt word perfect and accent perfect to the disbelief of the teachers, adults, students and crew around me. We were transported to France. I forgot my nerves and the language began to roll off my tongue, allowing me to speak with surety and confidence. It was an incredible day.

My classmates were already aware of my knack of attracting the unusual. On a school excursion the previous year, a photographer had requested my teacher's permission to take my photo. I was asked to model in the snow. I remember feeling quite embarrassed until my teacher explained that it would be good publicity for our school. After a lot of coaxing I allowed the photographer to take my photo. Much to my horror I was to discover the next day that he was a newspaper photographer and my photo was splashed across the front page of our daily newspaper. For a girl who likes to hide in the background and avoid attention, these experiences were daunting to say the least.

As a reward for dedication to my studies I was invited to accompany my teacher and ten grade four students to visit Noumea. I anticipated a glimpse of the atmosphere of France. The exploration of this part of paradise was scheduled for the September school holidays. Unfortunately, Deanna refused to permit me to go. She was frightened to let me out of her sight. Her continual fear was causing me to become quite disillusioned.

Fear slipped temporarily into the background as I experienced another life lesson two years later. My grade six teacher informed the class that she was taking votes for House Captains—one boy and one girl. Each child was asked to stand in front of the blackboard, and then every child could vote for their choice of captain. The votes were tallied and with an angry tone our teacher announced that I had been chosen to represent the girls. I was quietly overjoyed until I witnessed her look of horror. She had not anticipated this outcome at all, I was not her choice and she had every intention of showing me her true feelings. Her choice was my best friend Rebecca. Rebecca's mother was our music teacher and my teacher's personal friend and confidante.

Family values had not prepared me for the cruelty others could inflict, or the social standing that exists between the unenlightened. For in reality this is an illusion. Our world, unfortunately, reflects these social structures as real and we live by them accordingly, especially if we have a need to fit in. At twelve years of age I knew that material possessions—or the lack of—were not going to define me or stop me from expressing the love that resided deep within my heart. It did, however, cause me intense pain experiencing the jealousy of others and the emotional and mental darts they inevitably throw.

High school experiences I welcomed with pleasure and pain. Pleasure as my figure developed and thankfully Mother Nature organised my anatomy in the relevant order. She was more generous in some areas than others and I endured this phase feeling uncomfortable with my curves and well-endowed breasts. It was at this time that music flamed my senses and the dawning that boys make great friends, that is, until they realise you're a girl! My bedroom wall was framed with pictures of my music idols—handsome, unobtainable, yet wonderful to look at just the same.

Of course during grade ten there were the inevitable parties. You've guessed it! I was not allowed to attend which emphasised my differences all the more. Many embarrassing moments emerged with the boys vying for my attention and I had to contend with jealousy from the girls. My friends decided that my lack of material possessions and non-designer clothes gave them good reasons to ask me to leave the sanctity of the group.

As I reflect, I wonder how any of us survive these early years, yet we have an inbuilt purity that allows us to cope with life's painful situations. This purity is called our soul. It pulls us through the wormhole of adolescence into adulthood. From birth to seven years we develop approximately forty-five per cent of our emotional conditioning. From seven to eighteen we develop another fifty per cent. As adults we have only five per cent to work with. Oh dear! I was in deep trouble. However, there is hope. We can access the soul and heal. The healing comes later, much later with still more lessons to learn. Ah yes. There are still more lessons ahead.

I graduated from high school distraught at the thought of leaving behind a time of scholastic stability. I was not ready to become an adult, and face the world. It was sink or swim. The image of the Titanic loomed very close indeed.

But survive I did and enrolled at college, passing three pre-tertiary subjects the first year. My interest was formulated in Psychology, and in particular, relationship counselling. The challenge to understand male sexuality beckoned. Needless to say, Deanna was upset. This subject was deemed inappropriate for a young lady. I approached teaching as my back-up plan and for the first time my life began to move peacefully in the right direction.

But that too was about to change. In the second year of college my father James died. I was seventeen at the time, hoping to establish a relationship with him in the future. Unfortunately, lady luck with her fated deck of cards struck and I would never have the chance to accomplish this. In private, I grieved for the father I had never known, assuming the façade of a brave face while withdrawing internally.

Due to Deanna's sensitive financial situation she couldn't afford to pay for my education and it was explained to me that I was now required to support myself financially. My foster-brother Allan, who managed a local furniture store, casually mentioned that he needed to employ a Credit Officer. I accepted the position with gratitude and relief.

Destiny opened her heart. With this new dawning there would emerge the most intense life lessons to learn. This course of lessons would take twenty years. Yet, within the suffering and pain I would access my soul and find the most precious jewel of all. It was now time to meet my husband. I believed I was leaving behind a life of loneliness, and entering a world of love, peace and harmony which would provide my children with the opportunities I had been denied. I was adamant that I was going to break the chain and set in motion a new generation. Little did I know how accurate this would be, and in ways I could never have expected.

To Have and to Hold

At nineteen I met my husband Antonio. Within a year I was dutifully baptised Catholic and with this rite of passage a new chapter in my life emerged. Combining different cultures was always going to be tricky. My main concern was to provide my children with the stable biological environment I had been denied. I would never force my opinions on them; only provide a duty of care.

Antonio's parents Alberto and Maria were welcoming and gracious when we were first introduced. I was the talk of the family tree, with all of its members vying for information. An invitation was extended to attend a family dinner, to which Antonio's cousin Josef and his wife Elena were also invited. Immediately I felt at ease with Elena. Her almond brown eyes revealed compassion for the secrets contained within this family. Elena was a country girl at heart. There was much laughter and light conversation during dinner, with everyone feeling relaxed and happy. As we left the restaurant, Elena linked her arm with mine and said, "Welcome to the family." I had been given the stamp of approval.

An interrogation into my past commenced in earnest and details of my humble beginnings and my family's past emerged. Antonio's mother was distressed. Of course, I was labelled a gold digger, intending to lure their only son into my sticky web of deceit and I was accused of wanting to steal the family jewels and the wealth that Antonio would inherit. The truth was so far removed from their insinuations and innuendos, as I wanted and expected nothing.

Two tumultuous months later we were graced with temporary breathing space. While Alberto and Maria visited family and friends in Europe, Antonio and I lived together, happy and contented. These precious moments of borrowed time vanished when eventually Alberto and Maria returned home from Europe, praying that I was just a mirage in Antonio's life. Reluctantly, I went back home to Deanna but missed the freedom I now treasured. Antonio was a gentle, considerate and loving man and had convinced my family that as a couple we were truly blessed. Our joining was described as a blessing made in heaven.

After a few months we decided to rent a flat and live together. Our plans included allowing life to unfold and to live fully in each moment. I was ecstatic. Antonio discussed our plans with Alberto and Maria and they were bewildered. They had presumed their only child would not leave home until after he was married, and then expected that he would move straight into a home he had purchased. The salaries we were earning provided adequate income, but I wasn't convinced that we were prepared for the added responsibilities. I was disliked by Maria, although at this stage the words remained unspoken. Her feelings were screamed at me in emotional whirlpool blasts of energy. Not wanting to get involved, Antonio preferred to hide in the background, oblivious to the frustration unfolding around us.

Unable to tolerate the strain any longer, I tentatively broached the subject of marriage with Antonio. He concluded that his mother may have a point. Antonio was unable to face his parents in an act of defiance so he was only too pleased for me to shoulder the responsibility. He quickly agreed that we should get married. This was not the romantic proposal I had envisaged, but it was a proposal none the less and a date for our wedding was set.

Contempt is born of hatred. Maria confessed that she really disliked me because I was deemed unworthy to love her son. This was to be my crime for the next twenty years. On hearing the news of our engagement Maria formulated a strategic plan for a mighty battle. For six years she had introduced Antonio to respectable, suitable girls of impeccable breeding, and of families suitable to blend with her social standing. Beneath her looks of disgust I could sense the boiling rage that seethed within her and pumped through her veins, and yet a knowing settled upon me and I peacefully accepted the situation, unable to stop the inevitable path my life had taken. Antonio and I had issues to learn and resolve and higher paths to climb.

The seventh of March 1981 dawned. I stared at the white lace dress hanging on the back of my bedroom door. Designed with a six-foot train, lace-draped sleeves and a princess neckline, it was pure fantasy with a satin underlay and the beautiful lace that young girls dream of. My wedding day arrived with hair appointments and flowers to adorn the pews of the church.

As Charlotte and I entered the church to set up the flowers a feeling of profound connection flowed into my heart. The love of God was being buried deep within. My own crucifixion would take place at the appropriate time in the future. We were finished within an hour and we sat for a few moments, admiring the rainbow of colour and smelling the beautiful fragrance that now transformed the church. As we turned to leave the church an uneasy feeling stirred in me. Then a soothing whisper of love swirled in my heart and I steadied my nerves, knowing that I must endure the path my life was now taking.

The afternoon passed quickly. We laughed together, enjoying my final moments as a young single woman. Finally, it was time for us to dress and prepare for my wedding. Once dressed, one last addition was a pair of satin horse shoes for good luck. I felt like a real-life princess. All too soon it was time to leave. I needed to get to the church on time.

As I entered the church Charlotte stopped, turned to look at me and burst into a tirade of tears that lasted for ten minutes. The Catholic priest attending the ceremony proceeded to the back of the church to question the reason for the delay. Feeling the pressure of the future that lay before me, my sister was unable to control her emotions. They say that ignorance is bliss. I will be eternally grateful. I have been blessed with a strong, stubborn, defiant disposition when faced with adversity. My resolve would be tested many times in the years to come.

Charlotte calmed down and the wedding ceremony commenced. My foster brother Neil had accepted the honorary role of giving me away. With trepidation I glanced at Maria. She was wearing a grey dress that shimmered like a petticoat and her face radiated beauty, emitting a youthful glow. Her heart, however, was cold and stony like ice. Maria's dress screamed her denial that was shadowed against the silhouette of the union she preferred not to be. All too soon I heard the priest announce that Antonio and I were man and wife. Our destiny was sealed and the long haul to sanity was ready to commence.

My wedding was the first wedding I had been allowed to attend and I found the ritual incredibly daunting and uncomfortable with the eyes of so many people looking at me. Many years later I would be told that some of Antonio's family members were placing bets between themselves, predicting the duration our marriage would last. Most of them predicted that we would be divorced within a year.

The never-ending photos were finally concluded, champagne consumed, speeches spoken, feast partaken, and it was finally time to leave. A large circle was formed as custom dictates. I began to walk around the circle and as family and friends hugged and kissed us, they were bountiful with good wishes. As I approached my mother the tears began to flow. I just wanted to stay in her arms for just a few minutes longer.

Just before Antonio and I waved goodbye, Maria approached Deanna. She informed my mother that I was her family now and that she would dictate the outcomes my life would take. My mother's face turned white as she witnessed the full impact of the control that would encase me. She smiled at me, urging me to leave, indicating that everything would be fine.

The next morning Antonio and I embarked on our honeymoon. We both love the beach so we ventured to the sunny East Coast of our island paradise for seven days of tranquillity, soaking up the sunshine. Antonio had a terrible fear of flying so we stayed on our beautiful island instead of going to another exotic location. The weather was warm, providing us with the relaxation that we so desperately needed. Words remained unspoken; something wasn't sitting right between us. Quiet and withdrawn, Antonio was physically present but emotionally and mentally unavailable. I reasoned that the wedding preparations had taken their toll. We returned home with a quiet distance sitting securely between us. The distance would brew into a terrible storm that would be eventually unleashed.

The honeymoon was over and it was now time to return to the outside world. Alberto and Maria had purchased our first home. The foundation federation style house needed repairing. They spent every weekend for six months painting and refurbishing it. We were finally ready to move in.

I was to be taught the first lesson of family life. Alberto and Maria held control of our lives in their hands. If I offered an opinion I would be ignored and emotionally stomped on until I quietly stepped away. Maria and Antonio selected our furniture together and I entered my first home with her energy surrounding me daily.

During the next six months we settled into married life. A few months later I returned home from work to find that all of our wedding gifts had been removed. The cabinet in the kitchen in which they had been displayed now stood empty. I questioned Antonio, speaking in hushed tones. He looked at me in bewilderment, like a child whose hand had been caught in the cookie jar and explained that Maria had visited our home during the day and packed them into boxes, declaring that I didn't deserve them. I looked at Antonio with disbelief. I also remember my heart closing, as if a knife blade was sitting inside my chest.

During the early days of our marriage I had no idea that Maria would hold onto the disappointment and anger she felt regarding our marriage. I was still settled within the confines of my sheltered upbringing. But in that one moment it occurred to me that I would never be accepted by Maria, just tolerated to placate Antonio and Alberto. The treasure I have money cannot buy. It is purity of my heart and soul. Maria's gifts of material possessions to the children would be allowed for simple reasons, but she would never find a place in my heart and so the battle began.

At this stage in my life I didn't know how to forgive or see the bigger picture life was trying to teach me. I only knew how to endure the pain of hurt and suffering. In reality, my family heritage did match the high calibre of social and cultural standing that Maria searched for but the gambling debts and laziness of my great grandfather had taken our livelihood and forced us to live in the poverty we had endured. Many times I tried to explain this to her but her disbelief remained strong. The accusations were fixed, just like the pretend smiles. The emotional barbs would continue, and they did, every time we met.

I would discover that Maria and Antonio shared the same temperament. He had started to unleash temper tantrums of fury and anger unequal to anything I had seen, filled with fury and bitterness, volcanic in eruption gushing forward words of degrading intent.

Mental abuse became part of my daily life. There was no forewarning. The trigger point wasn't obvious to me. In the meanwhile I was living in inner and outer turmoil. Antonio had retreated into an inner shell of oppression and pain. At this stage I believed that I was doing something wrong to arouse his temper so I endeavoured to radiate as much love to him as possible. Sadly, this never seemed to be enough.

Placing no demands on Antonio, I gave him most of my weekly wage, requesting only a small amount to pay for personal items and clothes. He continued to fritter our money away, unhappy if he wasn't spending money or extending our house. I blocked the pain by retreating into my inner soul world. There I was loved beyond measure. My emotional and mental health started to suffer, and the reflection of sadness always hovered below the surface of my smile. Why did I need to endure this pain? I couldn't fathom that my loving heart couldn't reach or heal Antonio.

The full impact of the erupting volcano occurred unexpectedly twelve months after Antonio and I were married. Dinner had been prepared and I was watching television, hoping to relax and unwind. I had left my role as Credit Officer and was employed as an Assistant Accountant at a finance company, and the thrill of balancing numbers was rewarding. The chaos of end-of-month reporting figures were being constantly tossed around my head. Without warning Antonio began to scream, yelling abuse. He threw my dinner across the room. I watched in slow motion as it hit the kitchen wall, and Antonio continued to scream.

Staring at the wall in disbelief, I felt like I was in a bad dream. In slow motion the scene was still unfolding. Antonio demanded that I clean up the mess he had made, screaming in rage that I was to blame for upsetting him. The intensity of the situation seemed to ease so I quietly set to work to clean the kitchen. Within half an hour I returned to the lounge room to watch television. I was hungry, but also scared so I cooked two pieces of fruit toast. Breathing slowly, I stayed quiet.

Without warning Antonio started screaming again. He stormed into the lounge room and forbid me to watch television and demanded that I sit in the dark and think about my actions. What actions? After a busy day at work, I was tired, too tired to think clearly. Antonio stormed out of the room and turned off the light. As I sat in the dark room, the walls seemed to expand as my heart pumped, the whoosh of blood pounding in my ears. I was scared. Scared of the ferocity of his anger and temper, and not being able to fathom what I had done to hurt him. It was difficult to breathe and my chest hurt. His anger and temper raged once more. In hushed tones Antonio was threatening to take my life as I slept, promising that I would not see the dawning of the next day. He also threatened to hurt my family if I left our marriage.

I couldn't fathom the energy he had unleashed—it felt like he was a monster at times and yet I knew it wasn't the man I loved. It would take many years before I would realise that I wasn't the problem. Antonio's fear was the cause of his pain and suffering. Eventually, a man, in the form of a healer, would grace our lives but not before I endured more pain.

As I sat in the stillness I remember the sound of Antonio's snoring. As he slept I prayed that sleep would fold him in her loving arms. The only time Antonio found peace was when he slept. The sound of snoring would be embraced for only then did I know for sure that I had survived. The glory of another day was mine.

Connecting to my higher source of love emerged as I faced my fears on a regular basis. I overcame my fear of death, she emerged as a friend that I would see and feel. Of course, the following morning Antonio would apologise and promise that it would never happen again. And, of course, it wouldn't happen again, until the next time. We would experience months of relative peace between episodes and I would lapse into the lull of a false sense of security, only to have my emotions swaying on a roller-coaster ride of stupendous proportions as I continued to grapple with the intricate meandering of his mind. It was difficult to fathom its direction, intent or purpose.

When we experienced the quiet lull, peace prevailed until the volcano, filled with fury and rage erupted once more. Antonio would become amiable, docile even, and I would glimpse the essence of the man I had originally loved. I honestly believed in my heart that I could abstain from the actions that created this nightmare, certain that he would then return to the gentle man I knew he could be. I pleaded with him to visit our family doctor and seek medical treatment. The fits of temper were the cause of an imbalance, of this I was certain. He refused, firmly believing that the medical profession would institutionalise him for his behaviour and antics.

Initially my family members were not supportive when I explained the difficulties I experienced with Antonio. They also refused to believe that he was capable of these horrendous split-personality outbreaks, convinced that I was exaggerating the situation. I knew something was very wrong. His temper tantrums were not normal.

My resolve to obtain a solution remained strong. Not prepared to concede defeat, I thought seriously about having children. I believed in the goodness of Antonio's heart. The monster only emerged on occasions, so I reasoned. When I initially questioned Maria concerning Antonio's behaviour she looked at me as if I had taken leave of my senses. She denied that he had ever experienced problems, her words lashing at me like the sting of a whip.

During the spring of 1982, with no pre-planning, Luca was conceived. While shopping for groceries I tentatively broached the topic with Antonio. When I mentioned that my menstrual cycle was late and that I might be pregnant, he replied that he hoped I was joking. My heart sank to the floor. This was not the reaction I was expecting at all. I would never become used to the snake-like hissing of the anger that lay within him. It would always bite me when I least expected it.

Once my pregnancy was confirmed Antonio was concerned for three days. He demanded that I tell his parents, dreading the tragic reaction he was expecting from them. I found this concept difficult to understand as my family was welcoming and children were lovingly accepted—all children. Honesty is always the best policy. During lunch the following Sunday, I informed Alberto and Maria that they were going to become grandparents. Alberto was delighted. He started to show me respect and gentleness much to Maria's annoyance.

Once his parents had accepted Luca's impending birth, Antonio relaxed and I was astounded to find a paternal side to his nature. He was caring and concerned, mindful that I rest. Often I would wake from a nap to find him talking to my tummy, while bonding with our baby for those few precious moments each day.

Luca arrived into the world on a bitterly cold day in June 1983. I experienced post-natal depression, was tired, fearful and had slept little. Antonio would hold Luca, but never really participate in his daily care until he was six months old. Until then I flew solo. When Luca was twelve months old I was re-hired part-time. I accepted the position with open arms and found that interacting with others was the key to my sanity, making me happier as a mother and as a woman. Surrounded by people who treated me with kindness and respect, it was also my link and connection to the outside world. The experience of normalcy provided my anchor within the grid of humanity.

As I settled into my role I tentatively spoke to those I trusted concerning my issues with Antonio. I wasn't looking for blame, just hoping and wanting to find a solution. I craved the biological connection for my children that I had been denied. This was important to my sense of well-being. My commitment to find a solution remained strong. Running away from a problem is never the answer. The idea of having an affair with another man never crossed my mind or entered my heart while I endured years of loneliness. In the meanwhile, Antonio pursued his bachelor lifestyle, leaving me alone for days on end. When I questioned him concerning this he would explain that he needed to be alone. The darkness that shone from the depths of his eyes conveyed the inevitable look that demanded my silence. Abruptly the conversation would end. It didn't make sense at all. Eventually, I kept quiet, and endured our marriage yet feeling very much alone.

When Luca was thirteen months old the inevitable volcano erupted again. Unable to stand the situation any longer, I packed my belongings and waited for Charlotte to arrive and take me home to Deanna. Alberto and Maria had purchased our first home so it legally belonged to Antonio. They consoled him, convincing him that I would have to return.

Within a few days Maria phoned me to talk about the situation. She informed me that she was going to take legal action and fight me for custody of Luca. I had two choices. Return home to a life of cruelty with Antonio or raise Luca in the poverty I had been born into. Was there a choice? Yes there was, but I didn't take it. Instead of believing in myself, my strength and my capabilities, I surrendered to fear. I was just too frightened. Maria was triumphant; she had won her first battle. I cried myself to sleep.

I returned home to Antonio resigned to the fact that if I stayed married to him, I could protect Luca. I had visions of him following the path of his father and grandmother and was determined they were not going to be the victors of this war. They continually fought battles with my emotions, but I was adamant that the final outcome was going to be positive for my son.

Six months later I developed endometriosis, a debilitating disease that allows the lining of the uterus to grow in other areas of the pelvis. My gynaecologist explained that if I wanted to have more children I should consider doing so quickly. Marc was born the following year and Bella arrived eighteen months later. My family was now complete and the love they provide nourishes me always.

Once the children were born I started to revel in my role as mother. My ties to Deanna developed and our love deepened. This nurtured me as a young woman, keeping a steady hand on my sanity. Yet, I always sensed a part of my essence was missing. The unthinkable in my life then occurred. Deanna was diagnosed with lung cancer. My fear was beyond comprehension as I faced the prospect of losing my best friend, my anchor. It was then that my spiritual awakening stirred. I put down my Catholic Bible ready to claim my true spiritual inheritance. My life had to change!

Angelic Intervention

The awakening of Divine Union stirred the very depths of my heart. He walked into the kitchen of my workplace and the room began to fill with light. Andre was blonde, green-eyed and blessed with the face of an angel. I felt as if my existence was measured by this encounter. I knew this man! The knowing settled deep in my heart. Time as we know it, stood perfectly still.

This encounter was the beginning of our connection where I opened my heart to true love. In opening my heart to love I opened my heart to life as I danced and experienced the heady days of the adolescence I had been denied, much to my mother's concern. My visions were enhanced. Colour danced everywhere, glistening as golden rays reflected against aqua pools of crystal water. I believed that I had been rewarded for my patience and that indeed angels were smiling upon me.

Many years would unfold in the tenuous touch of time before destiny would permit me to explore this precious new love. Antonio and I were sharing his surname only, but he still haunted my sleep with constant reminders that I was still very much under his control. He no longer pursued me, but kept a vigilant watch over those I loved. Antonio used me as the vent to express his pain and frustration. On numerous occasions he used me as an emotional punching bag. He only saw the futility of it all in the times of reflection when the pain and suffering was sitting upon my shoulders. The volcano was a steady release valve for him. I held onto sanity by the whisper of a thread.

Once Luca, Marc and Bella were all attending school I started working full-time which enabled me to provide them with private school education. They were able to achieve a sense of familial life within the community of the Catholic faith. Primary school education opened the door to friendships with students and counsel from teachers whose guidance, love, support and companionship has been regarded as a highlight. Outdoor education enabled them to visit many beautiful towns and cities in our beautiful island, creating memories and experiences that have been locked in their hearts.

The children realised as they matured that their father loved them deeply, albeit in an obscure manner at times and it was never expressed. During this period, I embraced the role of master of illusion. I became the queen of disguise and we pretended that our family was living a peaceful existence. We did experience times of reprieve, but these times were short lived until the inevitable explosion of the next erupting volcano.

Particular work colleagues offered solace by reaffirming my sense of normalcy. The manager of our city office expressed a sweet natured disposition that was a soothing balm for my lonesome soul. During our animated conversations he would sensitively express the love and reverence he felt toward his wife. He became a conciliator for my battered heart, offering me a ray of hope that not all men were lacking in the warmth and sensitivity I needed.

Andre and I formulated a plan to share our allotted lunch times together. The connection between us blossomed and was evident to those viewing from a distance. He would allow me to sit on his plump leather chair while I ate my lunch. I felt as if he had given me the keys to his kingdom, the rite of passage to his throne. He was always mindful in his words and respectful in his actions toward me. I was impressed by his integrity. He lavished me with his time and devotion; it was beautiful watching the bud of our divine love unfolding. But I wasn't prepared to pursue the attraction, fearful of Antonio's reaction if I voiced my desire to leave the shell of the marriage that existed between us.

However, unseen angelic intervention forced me to evaluate my life direction. During one lunch break when staff members were busy with end-of-month accounting reports I offered to collect their lunch orders. As I drove to the delicatessen a beautiful love song played on the radio touching the depth of the connection that was unexpressed but stored in my heart. Outside the traffic was congested and I slowed down as the traffic lights turned red. A young man in his early twenties, travelling at an excessive speed, slid around the corner. He was watching the river, and unaware that the traffic had stopped, he didn't see the line of cars until it was too late. I remember thinking that I hoped he would slow down, and that if he didn't someone could get hurt.

The driver hit the back of my car and propelled three cars into each other. My neck nearly dislocated from my shoulders and my lower back screamed in pain. The doctor's diagnosis was severe whiplash and lower back trauma. I was lucky not to sustain any permanent injuries. Two weeks was predicted as recovery time, two weeks to sift through my thoughts.

Confinement has a way of opening the wounds of the heart. During the weeks of confinement I seriously contemplated the direction my life had taken. My mother was in hospital having her first operation to have a section of her lung removed. The biopsy had revealed a malignant tumour. I also realised that I could have been seriously injured in the car accident. Was someone or something trying to secure my attention? Love now permeated every cell of my being so I decided that it was the appropriate time to take a tentative look. Tentative it would prove to be. I procrastinated for days without finding the courage to talk to Andre. Where would I start?

Questions swarmed around in my mind like busy bees hovering over a honey pot. What is true love? How would I know? I had no tangible experience. Concerning aspects of love I was like a baby wobbling to master its first steps on solid ground, precariously unstable. My situation was sensitive and complicated to say the least. I stopped procrastinating and decided to talk to Andre. During the next few days we talked honestly and openly as I explained the lack of love I received in my marriage. In intricate detail I explained to Andre about Antonio's anger, but like most people, Andre could not believe that Antonio could treat me so harshly, and he too fell into the web of illusion we all seemed to be caught in.

Two months later I finally accepted that I didn't want to die before I experienced the sacred reality of divine love. At this point, I knew nothing of its experience only of its existence. For the next year I tentatively opened my heart to express the precious jewel that paved the path within. Antonio became a distant memory. I had endured eight years of abuse and loneliness while exploring every conceivable solution to save my marriage. It was time to concede defeat and allow my heart to lead the way! The joy and happiness I discovered was boundless energy, inconceivable to my limited experience. When I was with Andre I felt so light and free. It was liberating for both of us.

It is difficult to express in words the depth of connection Andre and I felt and expressed as two people. We were one in heart, touching the soul of each other and exploring the depth of pure being of spirit. I glowed with love and contentment. My eyes twinkled like diamonds, my body was healthy and vital, and my soul was encased in a beauty that only divine love reveals, explores and radiates in awe. I danced within myself, and euphoria abounded as bubbles of bliss floated and touched everyone around me. My work productivity increased ten-fold and my life was gloriously free, expressing the depth of everything alive within and around me. I have heard others describe the sensation of wholeness.

Until experiencing divine love I had only glimpsed vague snippets of real life. Divine love encases the sensitivity of experiencing the truth of joy and the simplicity of living in the now of each glorious moment, which opens doorways to a life so uniquely beautiful that most people cannot imagine it ever happening to them.

I didn't love Andre in a body conscious way, nor was I in love with him. I was love, expressing the truth of this sublime existence, sharing the profound truth of this wonder with another human being. Our connection touched the depth of pureness and we were constantly awed and uplifted by it.

To my delight we began to date. Surviving alone in a barren wasteland had not prepared me for the beauty of sharing my life with this incredible man. Andre was lavish in kindness, in thoughts and deeds, our connection comprised of him sensing my feelings without having to be told. He purchased long stemmed red roses and beautiful cards that expressed how much he loved me. The look of pleasure upon his handsome face revealed that the simple sentiment of giving was as natural to him as the air that he breathed. Finally, Andre chose a special day to confess his love.

Love Sublime

Andre engendered great care in preparing a romantic evening, hoping his declaration of love would resonate in my heart as one of life's cherished moments. His effort was encouraged by the closeness we now shared. The thought of taking the first tentative steps toward intimacy, however, was initially a daunting task.

I had given birth to three children by natural means and I was nervous, conscious of my imperfect body. Having recently discovered the joy of exercise I enrolled at a local gymnasium. My elation knew no bounds as my muscles toned and behaved respectably. Mother Nature had graced my body with excellent skin elasticity. I had sustained only a few silvery stretch marks and pondered that maybe, just maybe, I could be persuaded to relinquish my clothes so that the eyes of another man could see my hidden treasures, and in doing so, we could explore our own treasure trove together.

I am not a prude by any means. I was never taught to love my body, thinking it should consist of long lean bones with only a meagre morsel of flesh required for its outside coverage. My foster family, who had image delusions of their own, encouraged this notion. Lack of self-worth was repeated for the duration of twenty years, so it created within my mind a false sense of familiarity of truth where I was apt to believe that the opinions of others were to be valued and respected, whereas my own opinions I simply ignored. Andre was ultimately faced with my phobias head on.

Making love initially proved to be the daunting experience I had envisaged. The first time was rushed. We decided, after years of deliberating to consummate our love, to relinquish our fears and allow Mother Nature to lead the way. Andre's eyes, openly expressing delight, revelled in everything there was to know and show about me. I was conscious of my curvy lower tummy and thighs and hoped I wouldn't scare him away. It was in this moment I discovered that we, as women, too often despair about our imperfections. Men, in general, are way more compassionate and open in exploring our female form, mostly with eyes of wonderment delighting in the valley and mountains contained therein. Each intimate moment would enlighten us to a doorway, an opening that would eventually lead us to a greater closeness in heart, body, soul and mind. Andre's gentleness and eager delight conveyed that I could share intimate closeness with a man and genuinely want him to reciprocate this closeness in return. I also discovered during intimacy a therapeutic effect for heart recovery, as our experiences created joy beyond our imagining.

Time, in increments, opened in majestic simplicity to an amazing life. With the dawning of each glorious day there evolved a unique world of new wonders to experience. I would marvel as our lives unfolded, realising that the divine love we shared was progressing in subliminal ways. With complete trust in each other came an intense freedom to delve further into areas of the sacred heart that aren't shared between couples experiencing conventional relationships. Even with our lack of understanding of the many concepts that are contained in Divine Union, Andre and I were acutely aware that we were privy to the beauty and secrets of sacred love.

A plan started to formulate in Andre's mind. He had reached a milestone in his heart knowing that he wanted to spend the rest of his life with me. Now was the time for Andre to confess the feelings in his heart and take our love to the next level. He prepared a romantic supper for two; champagne bristled with bubbles of froth. The champagne bubbles tickled my nose and I looked at the man I adored with cheeky delight. It was difficult to fathom that after three years of friendship our love was intensifying, showing no signs of sliding down the slippery slope of complacency. The weekends we spent apart were becoming increasingly difficult for us to cope with.

A glass of champagne was consumed and a light supper partaken, we were ready to embrace the treats of discovery. Only deepening exploration allowed true freedom and we revelled in each other's touch. Our intimate moments were revered as ours alone, yet we shared the energy and sacredness of divine love. Other people were caught in the wonderment of its essence. They constantly gravitated toward us, not knowing why. Divine Union was constantly emitting its own truth and beauty.

Holding me in his arms, Andre's heart was pounding as if taking long, purposeful strides beneath his chest. His green eyes twinkled like jewels and I was mesmerised by the intensity of his gaze. He inhaled deeply and softly touched the curve of my cheek, memorising the contours of my face, to imprint this moment upon his heart. He spoke three words. With deliberate intensity he declared, "I love you."

My mind was muddled as I tried to comprehend that for the first time in my life I was unconditionally loved by a man. So, of course, in my nervousness I replied, "Yes, I know." I already knew that he loved me. If he didn't, his hands would never have progressed past touching my knee. No. It was not the response he had been hoping for. My phobia in expressing my true feelings was all bottled up inside me. A witty reply was not forthcoming to my rescue.

Andre studied my face for what seemed like an eternity. Gently he explained that his confession of love was expressed in our quiet moments of afterglow. It was important to him not to confess his feelings while we were making love. His expression was an honest reflection of the intensity consumed in the deepest recess of our intimacy. The desire in his groin had connected to the purest connection of divine love in the core of his heart and mind. This overjoyed him beyond the physical sense, and the purity of that connection in our lovemaking overflowed into me. His description was deeply accurate and honest, hence my fear. I had made love with Antonio so infrequently and in a conventional way only. The intensity of the love contained in Divine Union was extremely difficult to understand and cope with at times.

During the next few weeks I could feel tension sitting securely between us. I still hadn't said the magic words. They seemed to circulate in my head, project from my heart, roll around my emotions, slip off my tongue and slide into oblivion. I was behaving like a baby, feeling vulnerable, sensitive and unsure. I was too nervous to honestly allow Andre to see the real me. What if the real me wasn't enough?

Unable to hide from the inevitable any longer I decided to jump without my emotional parachute. After a sensual session of afternoon delight I whispered the murmur of "I love you too," that emerged from an unknown space stored in the well of a sacred garden. His sigh of relief was intense, audible to the soaring connection of our soul essence still reverberating inside my body. I think I heard a celestial choir of angels sing, "Alleluia". His relief was palpable. Finally, he heard the words he had waited so long to hear. We planned to share the news of our relationship with our families. But first, I had something important to do. I needed to speak to Antonio alone.

Monday mornings usually evolve like every other day but this particular Monday produced an interesting twist in the tornado that was about to turn. Our company's Managing Director heard from a young work colleague that Andre and I were quietly pursuing a relationship.

He was furious. His blessing was not forthcoming regarding the idea of a workplace relationship. Andre and I did not work in the same office vicinity. I worked in Administration and he worked in Managerial Sales. We had planned to approach our director after we had waded through our own personal issues.

Hoping that time would provide the proof we needed to ease our director's concerns, Andre proceeded in panic mode and denied our relationship, deeming it to be platonically based. I looked at him incredulous that he would take such a tactical approach. My mother's face loomed larger than life. The prospect of telling the truth was still firmly entrenched in my conscious way of living. I was not comfortable telling lies as lies have a way of unravelling when you least expect it and they always leave the bitter after-taste of the humble pie that inevitably needs to be eaten.

Andre was required to attend a counselling session as part of his job description and I travelled home alone knowing on some level that consequences were inevitably going to unfold. Once again, I had given another person's opinion more validity than my own, which still bound me to the same lesson.

To our dismay we were to discover that our director would not share in our joy and that problems of insurmountable proportions would begin to emerge. Like most people, he didn't understand the sacredness of Divine Union. The question remained unspoken. Were we strong enough in the early tentative stages of our Divine Union to deal with the problems we faced head on?

After considerable thought, our director decided that if we were silly enough to pursue the idea of a workplace relationship then one of us would be forced to leave. Andre was confident that our director would see the error of his ways so we began a charade of half-truths and secrets. I was devastated, and only minimally performing the work duties I was required to complete. Andre suggested that we take some time apart to consider our options and I agreed.

We lasted one week without seeing each other. Andre's mood was tense and terse, so unlike his diplomatic funny effervescent radiant self. His heart ached, as did mine, to express the tenderness that resided within. We were blocked on all levels with divine love having no outlet of expression. Unable to stand the pressure any longer Andre called me at work and asked to see me that evening.

We agreed to meet in a nature setting that held special memories for us. My rational mind screamed its refusal and tried to avert my heart, body, soul and mind from participating. I felt strong and detached until I witnessed the man who I loved and adored shed tears that welled in his eyes and they spilled down his cheeks. I brushed away the tears of pain and frustration and Andre tried to lighten my heart. He spoke with authority and certainty of his determination to find a way for us to remain together. Our lives were not making any sense at all.

Andre leant across to kiss my hand. It still held the trail of his tears and as he did so, a dam wall cracked and a pervading mass of love that needed to be expressed, cascaded through us like the pounding of a waterfall thundering from a hundred feet above. Our need to experience the full impact of Divine Union had a mind of its own and we were willing recipients.

Andre and I were forced apart by the will of others but Divine Union still flourished and was being nurtured by our souls—the real inner us. Tingles of energy catapulted through us like the crackling of lightning. Once we were comfortable, a pervading mass of energy began to circulate. Kisses and touch revealed the euphoria of our soul connection. With our bodies close I felt my heart expanding. In increments, the core of my heart opened to my soul which allowed Andre's heart and soul access to mine. The sensation was purity, lightness of touch, and tenderness, yet extreme heat and connection. Energy, vibrating on my skin, began to surge with turbulent intensity. I remember feeling so light in my body, calm yet powerfully free.

Tenderly he entered me as surges of energy powering through him entwined within me. A sensation of merging abounded from a distant pull that seemed to be outside of reality. The surges of energy powering through us opened us up to the experience of an intense peak that we experienced in complete unison. This opening allowed a pure connection of heart, body, soul and mind. Absolute perfection, like the lapping of waves on a calm blue ocean, we lay bare in the caress of existence. We chose not to move but stayed close, just wanting to be near each other. Oblivious to the child we had created; we felt no need to find the cumbersome sound of words to speak of our experience. Once again, in increments, the resonance of vibration returned to normal and eventually it was time to leave.

A dark tunnel loomed to those around us. We were blissfully unaware in our state of rapture that we were going to experience more lessons. Life also had a plan quietly fermenting in the guise of a healer, a friend, who would heal my pain, reaching into the abyss of my being and return me kicking and screaming back to the life purpose I had been born to. Why didn't someone just tell me how amazing my life was going to be? Ah! But that would have been all too easy and what, do you think, I would have learnt?

Unchained Melody

Rarely will our life lessons follow the reason of logic. As I reflect back on the problematic interferences that were soon to unfold in our lives, I became consciously aware that human nature can be at times, cruel and uncaring. It was not evident to me that I owned the solutions to introduce positive changes to enhance my life circumstances. I am aware now, upon reflection, how I visualized the wanderings of my life, viewing the image like a leaf; an ochre autumn leaf, allowing the wind to persistently lift me to the highs and lows of the scenery contained therein. There seemed to be no rhyme or reason to the wanderings, no distinct pattern, just a maze of situations and circumstances; the never-ending circumstances that left a chasm; a deep cleft, disabling me to touch the real inner me. My true self screamed its defiance at my nonchalant attitude and blind acceptance of the tiny slice of happiness that ebbed and flowed its way through this unfathomable truth. I loved and cared for others but not myself. This was my true crime and I bow my head lowered in shame! I was not able to see the infinite simplicity of this profound truth for many years, and as the ochre leaf tumbled through the cyclic circle of life's repetitions, I located a key to access a doorway and consequently found that the love, gentleness and respect I bestowed upon others was as equally deserving for me. The question remained: Could Andre and I save our Divine Union?

The half-truths and secrets continued for several months. The deception revealed my inability to find peace and contentment, and once more I found the purity of our love slipping away from the original encasement of sacredness. Within this turbulent environment there evolved a knowing that Andre and I were living on borrowed time, snatching moments of connection to express our love that was neither lasting nor fulfilling. I convinced myself that this situation was of a temporary nature and that the final outcome I envisaged would heal the pain that had started to emerge. The future loomed constantly, convincing us that our desired outcome of marriage was the only true reality. The past echoed sentiments of constant interference from other people that we blindly chose to ignore.

The pressing time of the ever-present now eventually revealed the ultimate truth. I had conceived Andre's child. A child conceived with the man I adored produced thoughts of wonderment. It was now time to face reality, confession being the ordinance of the day.

Because Andre and I were immersed in a turbulent environment, the chasm of distance started to appear in our relationship. He began to experience intense moments of frustration with me. Our problems stemmed from intermittent occurrences. The sensations of love contained in Divine Union were so euphoric, almost surreal, that it was difficult to express in words exactly how I was feeling. The ability to articulate the nature of the euphoria and discuss it rationally with Andre was almost impossible. My lack of confidence and emotional suppression brought to the fore my obvious problems that unbeknown to me, would prove to be the catalyst for the battle that lay ahead.

Divine Union, when expressed in a relationship of divine love is a sacred union between couples. It is intensely personal with its ultimate destination residing in heart, body, soul and mind. The feelings of love that are normally expressed in a healthy relationship lay hidden during my marriage. The pain and suffering I endured created feelings of mistrust, fear and abandonment. I hadn't become aware of divine love's existence in my relationship with Andre, only that I was love. It was so frustrating to feel such intensity of emotion with no outlet of expression.

Due to my fearful emotional patterns I avoided telling Andre about my pregnancy for three months. I shared the news with my sister Charlotte whose firm conviction led me to see the logical perspective. Her advice was accurate; I knew she spoke the truth. Andre needed to be told. I was petrified that the outside influences of other people's opinions would sway the course of our lives. This could be the catalyst to destroy our Divine Union. Each time I formulated the words they would become lodged in my throat before I could voice the truth. After experiencing weeks of fear I concluded that I had to tell him soon.

Andre responded to the news of my pregnancy with elation, overjoyed and awed that I carried our child within my body. He was also hurt and confused that I had shared this amazing news with others before telling him, hiding the truth for so long. I could not convince him that his perception of my lack of faith and trust was embedded in my own way of thinking. The fear of the unknown was the conductor of my train veering out of control. Learning the skills of open communication was a luxury I hadn't been privy to. My life didn't have clear direction. It seemed to blur like a splotch of paint when it is thrown onto a piece of canvas. You cross your fingers and pray that it all works out.

After his initial shock Andre confessed that he wanted to share our news with family and friends. To my delight he presented me with the most exquisite bouquet of flowers, his sentiment on the card sharing his delight. I read and re-read the words as I hugged the euphoria to myself, unable to resist a peek into our future life. It waited patiently like spring bulbs, anticipating the burst of perfection as nature prepares to bloom. We decided that it was time to put our lives in order. Antonio had to be told. My fraying nerves indicated that this consideration was a top priority.

Facing one's fears can be confronting at the best of times. I asked Antonio to meet me at my family's home—to simultaneously tell him the news of my pregnancy and to ask for a divorce. I knew I had Deanna's blessing to do whatever I felt was necessary at this stage in my life. She had become fearful that my marriage would endure, believing that I needed to experience the Divine Union I had found. We were both concerned for Antonio's fragile emotional state. Her presence was a comfort to me, knowing that she was sitting in an adjoining room.

Antonio arrived and I tentatively opened the front door. He sat down and looked at me with eyes that conveyed that he was a man on a mission, and obviously there were important matters that needed his attention. I had taken a full breath of air and as I exhaled slowly, I informed Antonio that I was pregnant.

His eyes became dark pools that created the illusion of shadows. An incredulous look swept across his face. He stared at me for a long time and it felt as if we were in slow motion, seconds becoming minutes. Then his searing anger hit my heart, the sensation like a knife twisting within. Antonio was devastated. I had no idea of the depth of his pain until tears started to flow freely down his cheeks. My hope had been that Antonio would finally find peace in his heart and I thought he would find freedom as the removal of the shackles that bound us in our marriage set us free. I believed we could access the freedom to heal our heart wounds. This would unshackle us, and allow us to heal before we were ready to pursue healthy relationships with other people.

Antonio refused to acknowledge the words I had spoken. Believing in the sincerity of his convictions, he demanded that I hear his confession of love. However, I knew differently. Love is never deliberately cruel or unkind. The purpose of love is to enhance the lives of each other. Antonio had a secret. He was terrified at the thought of being alone. This secret was concealed in the corner of his subconscious mind and he was terrified it would locate his conscious reality. Should this eventuate he would be finally forced to recognise it. The fear consuming him allowed a mass of dark, dense energy to emerge. Later, havoc would be let loose and the snake would unleash its venom at will.

As his tears subsided Antonio and I talked for a considerable length of time. The important matter that had previously claimed his attention faded into the background and for the first time he sat quietly and listened. I explained my reasons for loving another man. It was liberating to formulate my feelings and the reasons for the events that had occurred. In honest reflection, Antonio laid claim to his part of accountability for the lack of warmth, love and commitment he had failed to invest in our marriage. Within his honest reflection I confessed my desire that our divorce could be amicable. We had the freedom to re-start our lives with renewed hope for the future and this would be beneficial for everyone concerned.

Antonio looked directly into my eyes, a cold steel grey glint pervaded through the normalcy of soft brown hue and I stopped in my tracks. He would accept that I had grounds for loving another man and he would accept that I had fallen pregnant unintentionally. But divorce? Had I taken leave of my senses? If we divorced, the inner terror—his shadow side—would surface and lash its tail of destruction and he knew he would be left alone to face his secret. No, that would never do.

Antonio raised his voice in anger and soon he began to yell. When Deanna entered the room, mindful to ensure my protection, he demanded that she tell me that I must not divorce him. She looked at him, her eyes filled with compassion, sensing the deep fear and dread of the loss threatening to consume him. Deanna was also aware of the depth of love I shared with Andre and conceded my future happiness was bound in Divine Union. With defiant intent I returned Antonio's stare unwavering in my decision, refusing to change my mind. I was not going to relinquish Divine Union or be threatened by him any longer.

Calm, joyous feelings washed over me and I knew that someone was encouraging my plans, providing me with a clear future life path. The worst part was now over. Antonio was aware of my pregnancy and the innocence of the child growing inside me surrounded my heart with love. Antonio re-coiled the snake-like energy of his shadow side—his pain body—for now and once again I was caught in the illusion of his quiet acceptance. He knew from the depth, width and breadth of the divine love that emanated from me that I would never relinquish it.

Andre, on the other hand was unknown to Antonio. One way or another Antonio was determined to destroy my Divine Union. The children were his and no one was going to make him face his fear. Antonio sensed Andre was an honourable man who owned a humble and sensitive heart. He was supremely confident that he would find Andre's weakness, his sensitivity, and purposefully destroy our Divine Union. Of this fact, he was adamant.

The Long and Winding Road

The lull proceeding the stormy turn of events lay cocooned in warm lissom hands. The blitz of the hurricane contained in Antonio's pain body was yet to bombard us with its intended velocity. We were all aware of the devastation it would unfurl, still, a sense of calm prevailed from the depths of infinite loving wisdom. The presence of infinite loving wisdom is permanently accessible and resides within each one of us. It is stored in the cavern of the heart of the soul—the secret garden that is our true essence.

This is the secret that can change our lives. This is the key that will restore our world and spark an evolutionary process to the greater heights our birth-right intended. Knowing and accessing this wisdom are the achievable outcomes derived like the two sides of a coin. They both contribute to wholeness in understanding and completion toward ascension.

Our birth precipitates the path that is pre-ordained to exist. The freedom of human choice, not soul understanding, blocks the path to the pure existence that is ours. The pain and suffering we endure while living on earth is attributed to the fact that we cannot access our Spirit—our Higher Self—at will. We have temporarily forgotten how to do so.

As I read extensively, I began my search to find people who emphasised this concept as their truth. In my quest, the introduction to major religions, spiritual aspirations and philosophies evolved. There is a truth that validates each one of these in turn, yet a knowing circulates deeply within me. I personally believe there is something more. This indefinable belief is encouraged by a loving presence, the presence I experience as personally loving and caring of me. This presence can be called God, Budda, Great White Spirit—any name that you feel a connection with. Gently I sit in silence and I remember a truth I have always known. To permanently access this infinite loving wisdom within—the God-Self—is to spiritualise matter. Only then can we become permanently realised while living on planet earth. We shall heal ourselves and all who chose to inhabit such grace. Knowing this truth is one thing. Finding the key to access this truth is another matter entirely. The key is located in the discovery of life; our loving presence waiting, eternally joyful in aiding us to find it.

During the fourth month of my pregnancy, I expanded and radiated a glow that expectant mothers emit, bonding with my baby who was growing rapidly inside my womb. I worked until the seventh month of my pregnancy, loving the sensation of carrying my child. My work colleagues fussed around me insisting that I take care of myself. Andre and I continued our exploration of love. He would hold me in his arms, embracing and connecting with our child, and we radiated a glow of pure love around him as he developed daily.

Antonio's life, on the surface, evolved quietly. The anger he denied festered and became infected with his inability to release pain from his shadow side. For months he formulated a secret plan. His mind reeled with endless possibilities. To the world he portrayed the image of a man caring and supportive of his children. In reality, he was hiding from the secret that constantly threatened him. His plan was foolproof. He knew exactly how to manipulate situations to derive the outcome he desired. His mother—in her role of guiding light and teacher—provided the living example to express its simplicity. At the same time, my hopes and dreams were still woven around the expectation of a happy family outcome.

Ever so slightly, the tide of change began to emerge. Andre experienced times of deep restlessness. We decided that I would relinquish my role as Administration Assistant. Andre's future advancement with the company was exceptional and due to his dedicated approach and genuine care, he was appointed Area Manager. I was content to find employment elsewhere.

Our director insisted on giving Andre extra work commitments. He became distant and non-communicative. My health and vitality started to wane and I began to experience panic attacks, waking in the middle of the night, frightened to be alone. Something was terribly wrong. When I spoke to Andre conveying my concerns he would allay my fears with kind, soothing words. The distance between us, however, remained. Emotionally he was living in a world far removed from the love and respect of our Divine Union.

Secrets have a way of emerging quite by accident. Lies on the other hand are pointless and destructive. It takes an enormous amount of energy to sustain their existence. The strain of deceit ensnares a trail of despair. Lies also leave a residual mess of sticky feelings that become virtually impossible to resolve. Andre had been lying to me for months. He was scared, feeling pressured to leave our relationship. Unbeknown to me Divine Union cannot exist in emotional turmoil and tangles of this nature. There were now enormous gaps of emotional issues in our relationship. Andre was holding on to our love by just a thread.

Lightning began to quiver preparing to strike in the wake of Antonio's temper. He had discovered Andre's sensitivity. Antonio's plan, now hatched, had taken shape in the formidable guise of recriminations and repercussions. He set to work to implement his plan and in doing so, bolts of lightning began crackling in our direction, preparing to unleash a storm.

In my sensitive emotional state of fluctuating hormones, I concluded that Andre's continual detached state could mean only one thing, that he had stopped loving me. I irrationally placated myself. The love contained in Divine Union needs to be expressed openly and honestly. The glory is in the sharing of deep feelings and being able to express them without fear, knowing the love is meant to be. Other people's influence had continually chipped away until the foundation of our love had weakened and then crumbled under constant pressure. I could not fathom why certain people deemed it to be their right to express a negative opinion concerning our relationship, manipulating circumstances to pull our love apart. It made no sense at all. I was not aware at this stage that it was part of a greater plan. I was in pain. The pain was the only thing of which I was certain.

Heavy rains, combined with lashing circular winds opened to reveal the full intensity of the fury embedded in Antonio. It knew no bounds, leaving a path of destruction in its wake. The plan Antonio had engineered consisted of emotional and physical harassment. Andre was mortified. This pushed against the grain of moral values, deflecting human decency. Antonio became the constant thorn in Andre's side. He was painfully aware of Antonio's existence every time he moved. Antonio became a stalker, following Andre to work, sitting outside his home, watching his every move. The emotional and mental strain within Andre's sensitive nature created unimaginable stress and strain.

Unable to tolerate the situation any longer Andre relinquished our Divine Union. He decided to resume the core values of his previous life believing this to be the answer. Inevitably I knew. Words were not necessary. Long before the harrowing words were spoken I felt the heartache, the death of our divine love. I wanted Andre to honour our love with the truth for I had told him in our early discussions that this one act of decency was all that I required. I waited for Andre to honour our love with the truth. Patiently, I waited. It never came. Unable to tolerate the strain any longer, I conceded defeat and requested a meeting with Andre to resolve the situation.

We agreed to meet and as I slipped into the front seat of Andre's car I realised with heaviness in my heart it would be the last time. I had already accepted that I would raise Lorenzo. The thought of raising four children alone was a daunting one, but I was determined to overcome the difficulties that lay ahead. Deanna's unconditional love was imprinted upon my maternal instinct and I was determined to do whatever was necessary to keep my family safe.

Andre and I exchanged pleasantries. He was his usual effervescent gorgeous self and for a moment I lost my nerve. The euphoria of divine love still resonated so strongly within me that I was tempted to throw caution to the wind. However, my sense of fairness and honesty prevailed and the conversation eventually turned to the topic of our future life directions. I waited for Andre to tell me that he had returned to his former life. I needed to hear him voice the words so that my heart would not be tricked into believing he loved me enough to stay and face the numerous obstacles that were strewn across our path.

My pain turned to anger and a false sense of pride pushed me into allowing him to leave our relationship unscathed. But what I really wanted was for him to reconsider and select Divine Union rather than conventional marriage. I wanted him to tell me that he loved me more than life itself and I wanted him to love and nurture the child growing inside me. Andre said and did none of these things. I allowed him free will to choose to love another woman, to share his life with her. I accepted the responsibility of ending our relationship. It just wasn't fair. We had only touched the tip of Divine Union's existence. A miniscule experience and my memories were the only tangible mementos I could keep.

His reaction was one of feigned anger and rejection, yet I knew the truth of his deception. He had allowed his fears to overcome his resolve, which affected our lives accordingly. He did not understand that he needed to resolve conflict and settle differences and he knew not of the conviction to stand and honour his beliefs. Instead, he succumbed to the wants and needs of others and put their happiness before his own. He didn't believe that he deserved to be loved unconditionally. He knew only of hurt, rejection and fear.

The sad fact is, that is what we all do. We all know too well the feelings of pain, loss and rejection. Each one of us has the ability to hide in the secrecy of our inner shells, covering the real us so that we learn only how to survive, too scared to venture into the realm of the heart and lay bare the soul, too frightened to experience pain again.

I returned home exhausted, numb, and tired of the stress and strain. Finally, the truth was known. It was not the outcome I had envisaged or expected, having believed our Divine Union would withstand every test and survive insurmountable odds. I cried an ocean of tears. My mind was unable to comprehend the facts, my heart unable to comprehend the brutal finality. The truth, however, I would somehow have to learn to live with. My heartbreak, emotional debris and the mental trauma of our lives were flung to the four corners of our existence in a devastating swirling mass. How were we supposed to clear and clean up the destruction that hurricane Antonio had unleashed?

Two weeks lapsed and I began to feel depressed, the feeling was suppressed anger. I was furious at Antonio and I was furious at his parents for enforcing their values upon us. Marriage till death do you part! Devastated and confused that Andre didn't understand Divine Union, I was desperately unhappy. My health deteriorated and the glow that had radiated within me faded. A test confirmed that I had developed gestational diabetes. I needed to take insulin to slow the growth of my baby and I was admitted to hospital until I was able to give myself injections of insulin.

It became obvious that I was unable to care for the children, I felt so tired and weakened. In my depleted state I allowed Antonio to return home to care for them, consoling myself with the fact that this arrangement was only temporary. Once I had given birth to my baby I would resume my duties and ask him to leave.

I tried so hard to be brave, believing that somehow life would settle. The pain of loss was constant. It produced a dark cloud that refused to allow the light of the sun to shine. I would play music through headphones providing my baby with as much comfort as possible, concerned that my heartache would become his and this thought pushed me toward belief in a calmer life.

On a cold mid-winter day in June, Lorenzo was born. I had ballooned in weight due to emotional turmoil. My once svelte figure was now ruined as I sustained the physical burdens of pregnancy. I also developed tags around my neck, a legacy of diabetes. Could life get any worse?

Yes, apparently so. I returned home after spending seven days in hospital. An infection had developed in the entry wound of the cannula inserted to induce labour. The pain seared when touched and I was unable to move my arm. Antonio helped with the daily care of the children as I healed slowly from the birth.

Lorenzo was a placid, delightful, angelic baby who shared our lives. The children were amazed by his presence and yet the depression lingered. I had informed Andre while I convalesced in hospital that I had given birth to his son. He was elated, expressing a need to see him, but declining to do so in the same breath. He was right. It was difficult enough coping on my own, seeing Andre would only have made matters worse.

The days stretched into an endless pattern of life and ritual. I found it difficult to raise myself from my bed. A deep, dark uneasy silence accompanied me. The uneasy silence eventually became a roar and I felt my sanity slipping away from everyday life. I awoke one morning to find a tunnel, a dark tunnel facing me. It had arrived to lay claim to my sanity. I succumbed, entering the tunnel hoping to find peace.

As I entered the tunnel I experienced an abyss of fear. My every known and unknown fear bounced off the walls. A slurping vapour appeared at the mouth of a black hole and I struggled to gain control. I could no longer stand this pain. The loss was piercing my heart and I was exhausted with the struggle of life.

I arranged for Charlotte to care for Lorenzo and promised I would return in a few hours. Luca, Marc and Bella were safely tucked away in their classrooms and Antonio was going to collect them at 3.00 pm. For hours I drove around aimlessly, unable to think or feel, the pain thumping in and around my head, unbearably restless. I decided that I wanted to end my life. I believed, in my pain filled state, that no one would miss me anyway. In reality, I just wanted the pain to stop. My family were very worried about my emotional state but at this stage I was beyond caring.

Rain fell softly reminding me of the silent tears I had shed and the times I had cried myself to sleep. By then it was dark and I felt a surge of fear that bounced off the tunnel walls. It escalated, pounding in my ears. The rain intensified and as it hit the windscreen tears gushed from my eyes and ran down my cheeks. The roads were wet and slippery. I drove down streets aimlessly, allowing the road to lead me to wherever I needed to go. I remember knowing that I needed to find a pole. I was going to crash my car into it and end my life. Then the pain would stop, and finally, I would be free.

As I travelled along a particular straight stretch of road, a soft love stirred in my heart and I began to see a vision. Through the mist I saw my children. Their hands were reaching out toward me, a halo of white light circled above their heads. This opened a floodgate of tears and I wept even more. The scene changed and I saw my children standing next to Antonio and Maria attending my funeral. Antonio and his mother were standing rigidly still, their solemn faces projecting incriminating looks. In that split second, I understood that if I died Antonio and his family would raise the children and bathe them daily in fear and anger. Then I saw the face of my beautiful baby son so much like his father in looks and gentleness, motherless and alone.

In that moment of lucid reality, I experienced the truth in understanding that we exist in eternal perfection. Our pain and suffering is to be used as a tool from which we can learn. Its role is to teach us how to appreciate the gift of life. We are encouraged to look for life's deeper meaning and to release the illusions that bind us to our earthly existence. We need to find a way to release our fears. In the presence of fear is the absence of love and in the presence of love is the absence of fear. In order to experience wholeness we have to release our pain and suffering so that we can experience the glory of life.

I was facing a crossroad with two choices. One choice was death, the other choice was life. I realised the futility of trying to end my life and in doing so, I made a conscious choice to live. I found my centre of gravity, acknowledging the reasons to look for and find the simple joys that accompany life. It was time to face my pain, learn how to love again and to acquire tools to actively resolve my life situations. It was time to heal and move forward.

The loving presence that I have known my whole life touched my heart and it expanded to a width beyond belief. An outer experience of the same presence of love merged in a simultaneous flow. My battered heart experienced the sweetest taste of the most exquisite love. I cried from a space within the depths of myself, starting to release the anger and resentment I had stored there.

As I drove home I realised that I had witnessed a sacred experience and that I would express a deeper loving kindness. I also realised that my dark emotional and mental tunnel was now filled with light. The love that Andre and I created as Divine Union evolved had changed me forever. I had become more loving and compassionate. I was now determined to honour my life and find the key to open the door.

Homeward Bound

The next seven years slipped into view on the horizon of a barren wasteland. I was still angry, fighting battles with Antonio, unable to forgive or to understand. Suppressed anger is a dangerous emotion to bury. It lays dormant while seething deep into the tissues of the liver burrowing deeper and deeper, scurrying into layers of delicate cells. The cells eventually become tired. If left unchecked, the anger can develop into a hardened mass as the imbalance struggles to be heard. Resolving the issue that caused the imbalance is necessary before it anchors into the physical body. Forgiveness is our saving grace. During the next seven years I would discover the depth of the anger I had suppressed. It would prove to be my teacher of numerous lessons. I would also awaken from the slumber of deep sleep to discover the joy of life and find the key to access the doorway that would reveal hidden truths. The lessons to emerge would be learnt the hard painful way, until a healer would enter my life. There would be a shining luminous light at the end of the tunnel to greet me. But first, there was still much burrowing to do.

I arrived home at 10.00pm and slipped beneath my doona. The comfort of clean, cotton sheets soothed me and I soon fell effortlessly into a deep dreamless sleep. Within an hour I awoke to the sound of my baby son crying, conveying his need to be fed. As he lay cradled within my arms his tiny head moved from side to side, his senses searching for the tip of my breast. Gulping the sustenance of milk that Mother Nature so bountifully supplies, he visibly relaxed in my arms and I gazed at his beautiful face. A feeling of contentment and peace pervaded my heart and I knew the worst was over. However, the battles with Antonio would keep happening.

Antonio believed that he held our lives in the palm of his hand. Satisfied with his handiwork, he viewed Andre's life and declared that it was now officially standing in a terminal mess of pain and devastation. Hurricane Antonio had left its mark. To the outside world, Antonio had taken on the role of caring father. His family were convinced that he was providing an amazing duty of care in these trying circumstances. They just didn't see what he was doing when left to his own devices. I continued to heal rapidly, convinced that I was ready to assume the responsibilities of motherhood alone. This was a major mistake!

After enduring a morning of intense verbal abuse, I informed Antonio that I was ready to resume the full responsibility of raising the children alone and I asked him to leave. There was the inevitable raised voice as scathing remarks, personally cruel and demeaning, ejected from his mouth. My emotions felt the inflicted wounds of the words that cut through my heart like welts from the lash of a whip. I stood my ground and demanded that he leave.

Lorenzo began to stir in his cradle and began fidgeting uncomfortably, sensing my panic. Even now as a young man he senses my pain. Antonio's temper hit full velocity and in a split second the snake unleashed its tail. China plates and crystal glasses crashed to the floor as he swiped them off the bench. He retrieved a hammer from the kitchen drawer and began gouging the leather chair—ripping the arms as he lashed out in full fury releasing this destructive force. Then his hand reached into the kitchen drawer and retrieved a long blade knife. I stood still, unable to move, feeling absolute terror as I watched the scene unfolding. He was a man caught in a maddening rage that had veered out of control. My heart was hammering so loudly in my chest that I thought it was going to burst.

The steel edge of the knife glistened as sunlight hit the kitchen window. I stood in horror as he held the knife, threatening to cause me harm. Lorenzo's cries were escalating and with the skill of an elite athlete, I jumped across the kitchen chairs to retrieve my baby and ensure our safety. With one arm I scooped him up and ran out the front door, not stopping to look back until we were safely at our neighbour's home.

Having reached the end of my tether, I knew it was time to leave. The resolve that accompanied this decision felt like the sense of coming home. I telephoned my sister Louisa. It was time to move to another state. I reasoned that having family members to love and support the move would uplift us. Moving to a new city and rebuilding our lives was initially a daunting concept. I was going to leave everyone and everything I loved behind. Still, I believed that it was time for us to leave.

I arranged to visit Louisa the following week, having made arrangements to leave the children with Deanna. It was imperative not to arouse Antonio's suspicions. I explained to Antonio that I was exhausted and needed time to recoup after Lorenzo's birth. Louisa arranged an appointment to see her lawyer, a young woman well known for her dedication and compassion toward helping women in crisis. I was feeling excited about our future direction.

At 2.00 pm I walked into the lawyer's office and my confidence bolstered immediately. I felt completely at ease. We discussed my current situation for a considerable length of time. She informed me that I could take the children and move to another state without Antonio's permission. However, once established, the law stipulated that I had an obligation to tell Antonio where we were living.

My eyes filled with tears and I began to cry. My mind comprehended the words she had spoken, but my heart didn't comply. I had envisaged that this would be our new start, our new beginning, and that the legal system would rally to my defence and help me to escape Antonio and the battles we faced. My life had to mean more that this never-ending roundabout of pain and suffering. I would not believe, nor accept it would only amount to this.

Why was I blocked at every turn? Why wouldn't Antonio's parents listen to me? I finally admitted defeat as I boarded a plane and returned home. For reasons unbeknown to me I obviously needed to stay. In times of frustration I would consider the fact that my life with Antonio was the only existence I would ever experience. Still, my heart was determined to experience my right to freedom and I was prepared to work tirelessly for it.

My new resolve anchored my heart to my love for my children. I knew they would mature to adulthood, and preparations were in place to leave Antonio at the appropriate time. I have always held the belief that my children are precious gifts on loan to me, for they have a journey of lessons to learn independently. My role is to love and support them in this journey. It is a privilege that I share with the higher loving presence in my life, from which we are all loved equally in turn. I would learn the lesson of infinite patience, biding my time until then.

During the next two years I built a fortress of armour around my heart. To the outside world I was friendly, compassionate and kind. Inwardly I was reserved and emotionally distant. The added weight I had gained gave me strength. It added to my sense of power and I refused to let it go.

In reclaiming my personal power, I invested my time and energy deciding how to be of service. Unconditional love resided in my heart. Men, however, were not privy to peek inside. I closed my heart to men, firmly shutting the door. The resonance of iron clanging shut reverberated around my now prison walls. It was my belief at this stage, that we are only given real love once in a lifetime. I had been given the blessing of Divine Union and I conceded honestly that I had failed. Albeit, I did acknowledge that the influences of other people had not helped our situation at all.

The clearing and clean-up stage of Hurricane Antonio then commenced in earnest. We rebuilt the shattered fortress of our lives with painstaking care and attention, and in doing so I started to reach beyond myself. I wanted to learn how to love others within a broader spectrum. How could I be of service? Could I make a difference?

During the re-building of our lives the arguments with Antonio escalated and his fear became more intense. He detested our re-building programme, furious that I had weathered the storm of the hurricane. He watched the love we shared with Lorenzo, but would not and could not accept that the essence of divine love had survived, and still lived in the heart and soul of the child I had conceived. He forbade it. This development was simply not part of his plan.

During the next few months I enrolled in an introductory computer course. I was conversing with another student when she informed me about her interest in a hospice care programme that immediately caught my attention. Allowing someone facing death an avenue to express their greatest fear and concerns was a service I was happy to provide.

The hospice volunteer course took six months to complete. As hospice volunteers we were respected and welcomed with warmth from the nursing staff. The patients—-in their greatest hour of need—I found to be warm and loving. Some were quite intent in hiding their pain and fears from their loved ones. They mainly feared they were being a nuisance to all concerned. We also provided a reprieve for family members, allowing them to rest from the strain of providing constant support and care for hours on end.

I had faced fear repeatedly, so I felt a kindred affiliation for the patients I met. I also noticed a connection of spirit as death of the physical body beckoned. The obvious question asked when facing death is a query of the existence of eternal life. I would be given a first-hand experience with a patient called Henry.

Henry was a gentleman is his early seventies; such an amazing man, exuding a warm and caring nature. He had been recently diagnosed with cancer. When I visited him, he refused my offer to help him make his bed. I was asked to sit in the chair and wait until he had finished. He also insisted on combing his hair, putting on his slippers and dressing gown and then washing his face and hands. Finally, he would sit in the chair opposite me and talk to me about the details of his life. When I queried this ritual, Henry commented that I deserved the effort he made, suggesting that it was the least he could do for a lady. When I explained that it wasn't necessary, he just smiled and continued. My heart was humbled indeed!

I visited Henry for several months and during the last few weeks of his life watched with sadness as his health rapidly declined. One morning I approached the nurse's station for a report on patient's health and well-being and was informed that Henry was preparing for death. It was with a heavy heart that I approached his room.

As I entered his room a cold chill raced up the length of my spine. I looked toward the window and found to my surprise that it was shut. The temperature in the room returned to normal when Henry ushered me toward his bed. His face was tinged grey-blue and his eyes had sunken in his head. His breathing was slow and laboured. In a hoarse voice he whispered, "Move closer, I have something to tell you."

I moved closer to his bed and stood beside him. Immediately his breathing returned to normal. The colour of his skin radiated a healthy glow and his eyes shone sparkling and bright. Repeatedly, I blinked, thinking the lights were playing tricks on my eyes. He held out his right hand and put my hand onto his palm. The look of rapture filled the spaces of his weathered skin and his eyes shone with the brilliance of love.

I looked at him in awe, feeling the exquisite sensation of an inexplicable vibration on my skin. In a voice pure and strong Henry asked me, "Can you feel his presence?"

Before I could ask who he was referring to, Henry continued to speak. He said, "It's the Lord in our presence and he has a message for you." I remember thinking that he might be hallucinating when quite naturally he commented, "I am quite lucid you know." I decided to sit in quiet respect and allowed him to speak. Henry resumed speaking to me with gentleness, quietly, like you would talk to a small child, making sure they understood. "You are a messenger and have a specific purpose for your life. It is important that you do all that has been asked of you. Humility is your gift for you know the truth. The first-hand experience of a higher loving presence has been with you all of your life and in a future time the words will be written through you. The message is one of simplistic but profound truth immersed in a story that encompasses all aspects of love." Henry began to smile, a smile so knowing, so loving, filled with awe in his greatest hour of need.

The golden glow radiating around Henry's body continued for a long time. I sat with him and felt the presence of what can only be described as pure love. To my dismay a few hours later, his face had turned grey and his breathing once more became laboured and shallow. Then he fell into a deep sleep.

In my awareness there evolves an understanding that everything happens in our lives for a reason. Sometimes the reason is obscure, and sometimes it is very clear to see. The higher loving presence I have known all of my life reached into the physical world and sent a message I could either accept or ignore. Having access to this pure source of our higher loving presence is the truth we are all meant to know.

Henry died a few days later surrounded by his family and friends. He was not an overtly religious man, bearing no pre-conceived ideas of a heavenly abode, but lived his life as a man who cared passionately for humanity and treated others accordingly. His legacy and the memory of his humble heart I will treasure always.

Spending hours talking with Henry was a healing balm for my heart. He taught the lessons of kindness and respect. Very quickly I realised that Henry was a man who could see into the hearts of all people and he knew instinctively, that on the inside, I was hurting. The petals of my heart finally opened to the light of the sun and I smiled. This was his gift to me.

Opening the Gateway

The year 2000 arrived with fanfare. Spectacular celebrations provided the anticipated link to connect the heart of mankind. I viewed the dawning of the first glorious day as we shared the wonderment of witnessing the birth of a new millennium. Strewn across the sky was a hazy scarlet glow as the sun peeked over the mountain to take a glance at history unfolding in evolution's natural sequential grace. This new dawning held the hopes, dreams and wishes of all people connected to our family of humanity. It held the hope of world stability, it held the dream of a peaceful, prosperous future and it held the wishes of community love as we learn to accept the differences that divide us nation from nation.

It is time to remove the veil of concealed rose coloured glasses that try to convince us that as one person, we can do, and change, nothing. It is not the shadows of life that creates our greatest fears. What frightens us most of all is the brilliance of our light, the truth of how amazing and capable we really are. We can create remarkable differences in our lives should we choose to do so. The key that ushers us through the gateway will open to the command spoken by one who owns a humble pure heart, purity that shines forth with profound simplicity in truth. It is time to move forward and claim the birthright that is ours to inherit. Hang on. Help is on its way.

On the 5ᵗʰ January 2000, I was scheduled to have surgery. The gall stone attacks had been severe for several months. I was suppressing anger, galled at Antonio winning the battles he repeatedly created in our lives and frustrated that I couldn't reach the core of his pain that prevented us from moving forward with our lives. Suppressed anger had been burrowing for seven years and its effects had finally become apparent. My gall bladder was diseased and urgently needed to be removed. I had not found a resolution to the situation concerning Antonio. He was still creating havoc with no future end in sight.

As I approached the hospital doors, a foreboding feeling swirled in the centre of my stomach. The operation was scheduled for 2.00 pm and I was comforted by the knowledge that I would be returning home to my children in a few days. The operation proceeded as planned. A muffled voice was telling me it was time to wake up. The discomfort I felt was indicative that the operation had taken place. My diseased gallbladder and I had parted company and I was grateful that the pain of the attacks was now a distant memory.

Later that evening the surgeon walked briskly into my room confirming that the surgery had been a complete success. I was permitted to return home in a few days. He recommended that I rest and allow the healing to take its course. That was not going to be a problem, it hurt to breathe. Resting was a comforting thought.

The next morning a young nurse came into my room and indicated that she needed to remove the drainage tube. It was attached to the stump of my gallbladder. The exit wound of the tube was stitched to a tiny hole in the side of my stomach. Thank goodness that breakfast was still an hour away. She encouraged me to hold my breath and when she instructed, I was to breathe out quickly. The thread that held the tube in place was cut and with an almighty pull she yanked the tube from the stump.

The pain was excruciating. The drainage tube had hooked onto the stump of my gallbladder. Neither of us realised it had ripped when she released it. She was extremely apologetic but told me that its removal was imperative. I was left alone, everyone oblivious to the damage that had been done.

The pain had escalated during the day. The surgeon's assistant returned that night to check on my progress and when I mentioned the severity of the pain I was experiencing, he explained that it was normal to feel discomfort after an operation. He promised that I would feel better soon and could go home the next day if I wanted to. Intuitively, I knew something wasn't right, so I asked if I could stay another day.

During the night I woke with excruciating pain in my right shoulder, a sensation similar to hot coals being pushed into my chest. A patient in the adjacent bed pressed the buzzer to notify the nurse. Two nurses entered the room. Knowing looks of disbelief flowed from one to the other. They were convinced that I was overreacting until I mentioned the fact that I had given birth to my daughter without the use of pain relieving medication. The nurses left my room and consulted with the surgeon. He requested an ultrasound examination as a precaution, concluding that it was in everyone's best interest to make sure there were no complications.

At 11.00 am the next day I was wheeled into pathology. An ultrasound examination indicated that the stump of my gallbladder was bleeding profusely into my shoulder cavity, hence the pressure. I returned to the ward fifteen minutes later and found the surgeon waiting to speak to me. With a grave look etched on his face he sat next to me on the bed and held my hand. He explained that I was bleeding internally and that another operation was necessary to stop the bleeding. Oh no, not another operation! I was still coming to terms with the first one. As I signed the consent forms the doctor explained that I had peritonitis. If I had returned home when I was scheduled to I would have died in my sleep. The stump had become inflamed and infected. During the second operation the surgeon would stop the bleeding, cleanse the wound and bowel and I would be required to stay in hospital until I had received a course of antibiotics.

Once more, through the foggy strains of reality I heard the sound of a female voice and the resonance of a bell as pure as crystal. A tube connected to my nose was annoying me and I tried to pull it away only to be told by the nurse that it was oxygen as I was having trouble breathing. Surreal bliss was enfolding me in loving arms that I couldn't see. I was not registering any pain at all. For a moment I contemplated that maybe I had died so I asked the lovely nurse, who smiled and assured me that I was very much alive. A dose of morphine had been administered. My body needed time to heal.

Enduring two operations in three days was debilitating to say the least. My body reacted to the intrusion. I developed bronchitis, needing two courses of intravenous antibiotics and of course I had another drainage tube attached.

On the sixth day after the second operation it was decided that the drainage tube needed to be removed. The surgeon arrived to remove it, as the nurses were not prepared to try. Of course it was stuck and wouldn't move. He left, but promised to return in a few days.

During the night I woke with a start. I felt the sensation of a hand touching the wound where the drainage tube was connected. I opened my eyes fully to witness the image of blue light hovering around my bed. I strained my eyes to see the nurse who should have been standing there, and I realised to my amazement that there was no one there. The light shimmered more brightly, still hovering. I felt a tremendous pressure and energy around my neck and back. The energy was so strong that I coughed. Ouch! I really tried to avoid doing that. It really hurt as the wound and stump was so sensitive.

I felt as if my body was gently guided back settling onto the pillows. The tube was removed from the stump, and the pain had eased considerably. When the surgeon returned I knew for certain that he would remove the drainage tube easily, so I drifted comfortably toward the sleeping angels of love.

Two days later the surgeon returned, a look of sheer determination settled across his features. He knew I was feeling restricted and wanted to return home. Gently, the stitch that held the tube in place was cut and with the grace of a violinist, he pulled the drainage tube out with one clean sweep. I felt no pain or discomfort, just a sense of gratitude knowing that the ordeal was finally over. I was allowed to return home the following morning. After quickly eating breakfast and packing my bag, I waited for Antonio to collect me from the hospital. The door opened and there stood Marc and Bella, both talking animatedly about the happenings during my absence. Finally, it was time to leave.

As I walked out of the hospital toward the car I felt tired, drained and unwell, hobbling along the corridor at a snail's pace, much to the bewilderment of the children. This time I had not just looked at death, I had faced it by touching the fringed tassel of its reality. The anger I had burrowed had hurt no one but me, damaging my organs in the process. This experience five days into the new millennium was not a future I had envisaged. Life changes were put in place and the healer would appear very soon.

I arrived home exhausted, and stretched out on the couch to rest, too sore to move. Once again, Antonio was living with us. The children conveyed to me that during my stay in hospital his help and care of them had been exemplary. Aware that I had nearly died, he was shocked to witness the shell of my former self returning home and that I looked as desperately sick as I felt. His fear—the serpent snake of his pain body—hit his heart with full intensity. He knew there was only one way to restore his balance.

The sound of crockery hitting the kitchen was so loud I was forced to wake up. The inevitable screams had reached a pivotal point and the thumping of his fists hitting the bench reached my ears. He was hurling abuse at me for my lack of concern toward the children while I convalesced in hospital. For the past week he had fumed, terrified that I might die and that he would be left alone. Faced with the knowledge that I had approached death, the serpent within had touched the core of his heart. I needed to be taught a lesson, he reasoned, just in case I became sick again.

Because I was too ill to move, this particular display of anger from Antonio portrayed to the children the degree of their father's temper. Luca was seventeen and he reached into himself and faced his father with the truth of his lack of sensitivity and compassion toward me. Antonio was horrified. His parents, through their lack of discipline, refused to concede their son was out of control. They would not face their only son, for the truth was too much for them to bear. They reasoned that my lack of financial wealth was due cause for their son to treat me the way he did.

Antonio was educated at the finest private school and had been raised by parents who are upstanding pillars of the community. It was deduced that the problem must be mine as their son would not have committed these activities. I did not want Antonio hurt; I just wanted someone, anyone, to help us. My foster brothers contemplated the idea of hurting him physically but I forbid them to do so. Violence begets violence and I knew this was not the resolution I was looking for. There had to be another way.

Ignoring the devastation outside in the kitchen, I laid my head back onto the pillow. This was the first time I had been unable to make sure the children were safely out of his way. Too weak to telephone for help, I said a silent prayer to the angels asking them to keep my children safe. I fell asleep to be woken by a knock at the front door, followed by the vague sound of male voices. Opening my eyes, I saw two policemen standing in front of me asking me if I had been physically hurt.

Antonio appeared from the outer doorway of the kitchen and walked toward the policemen standing next to me. He gruffly assured them that I was fine. With slow deliberate sentences I explained that I was recovering from two operations and had just been released from hospital. Their look of surprise was evident. They studied the scene of devastation that was spread around them and asked Antonio to accompany them into the kitchen.

Antonio was spoken to at length concerning his behaviour. They indicated that I would need help and support to heal. While consoling him, they explained that they understood the pressure he was enduring. Antonio sat on the dining chair, his hands brushing his face in frustration. He was not used to anyone telling him he had behaved inappropriately. Luca had called the police in an act of defiance toward his father and as a consideration of love for me. He refused to tolerate the situation any longer, he was determined it was not going to continue.

The laws pertaining to abuse—emotional and physical—were changing, and abuse was no longer tolerated in the community, allowing police a greater avenue of intervention, ensuing safety for those who were being hurt. Change had been occurring gradually. Many new advertising campaigns added to the messages being presented. Luca had found his key. The children were aware that Antonio's emotional and mental stability originated from an imbalance and that he needed to seek medical assistance.

The two concerned policemen left our home after obtaining an assurance from Antonio that he was prepared to proceed in a calm manner and that he would care for the children while I healed from the operations.

It was at this time that I became consciously aware of two important things. The first was the reaction of calm and rational conversation Antonio entertained when the two policemen spoke to him concerning his behaviour. There was a way to reach him. I had finally found a key to access his inner self. My heart soared. The second realisation occurred upon reflection; I noticed that I did not react to Antonio in my weakened state. When I looked at the situation without judgement, I faced his pain body—his anger and fear—head on. Viewing him without judgement and with detachment, I looked deeply into Antonio's pain and realised that his pain and fear blurred his concept of decency. I also knew there resided within him a point of light that contained his spirit, his real self that was purely connected to the higher source of love—the presence that I speak of. All I had to do was find a way to retrieve it and restore it to life. This was a breakthrough. I had found the solution I had been looking for. Now all I had to do was to find a way to implement it.

The healing process of journeying from pain to recovery required six months of rest until my health returned to normal. During this time of recuperation, the guidance I received was comforting. The words were familiar to me, like a trusted companion, a friend, awakening the knowledge that was stored within. Knowledge is brought to the mind through the process of awakening. Wisdom, however, lies stored in the depth of the heart. It is the connection of the heart and mind, body and soul that provides a key to access the power within, which in reality accesses this higher loving presence.

Meditation is a wonderful avenue to access the depth of the soul and it exists in numerous forms. During regular intervals in my life I have experienced meditative sojourns where I tuned into other levels of awareness, connecting to our higher source of love. As a child I was not able to function in both realities simultaneously. As an adult I am able to merge the two, which enables me to walk with one foot in the spirit world while living a wonderful life in this world.

The healing of my body required times of rest and deep stillness. There was a gentle loving presence accelerating the healing process. I was not frightened of the presence; I chose to allow the healing to take place. It was calming and soothing, a completely natural occurrence, a remembrance of a time temporarily forgotten but lovingly accepted anew.

During the next few months I refused to become so affected by Antonio's tantrums. I attended structured meditation classes, delving into many intricate aspects of personal growth. This discovery was a stepping stone that would lead me along many paths until I arrived at my final destination and true purpose.

It was time for me to test the teachings I had received. Forming meditation classes designed for women led to devising a programme that enabled them to receive instruction—a way to utilise concepts and achievable life tools that would lead them to access positive change in their lives. The programme involved teaching others how to access their true self-awareness and in turn use these gifts to help others. Self-awareness is effective in teaching self-empowerment. The classes offered participants an opportunity to share their life experiences and find their true life purpose. For those who were suffering at deeper levels, I referred them to seek medical attention. My life was now starting to make sense.

Having a positive way to be of service opened my heart toward women and I developed many warm friendships. This non-threatening environment held a strong sense of security for us. Our closeness opened us to the avenues of honest communication, learning to access the confidence to share our feelings, and we were excited to discover that we were not alone in the drama of life. We also discovered the joy of sisterhood. Men were not allowed. Well, not just yet!

I had recently completed a six week esoteric course and found to my delight that the meeting room housed a wonderful library of literature. I was in heaven. The facilitator casually invited me to attend a lecture on healing. Initially, I said no, but then changed my mind. My daughter Bella accompanied me to the lecture.

The 9th of July 2000 was a bitterly cold mid-winter evening. Bella and I arrived at the centre and quickly found a seat. I turned my head to see a man talking to a group of people, and within ten minutes he stood at the front of the room. A massive glow of light surrounded his head and upper torso. Michael began to speak. Hushed silence fell upon those present as he shared his life experiences and the outcomes that had led him to facilitate his lecture. I noticed genuine warmth in his manner and as the lecture progressed, he portrayed a genuine desire to help people move forward with their lives.

On waking the next morning I heard a voice say, "You will visit this man when the time is appropriate and this healing will change your life." That may be so, but I was still a very long way from being convinced!

My Sweet Surrender

Surrendering to the beauty and transformation that accompanies the knowing of our higher loving presence is the true purpose that precipitates evolutionary life. During the next five years I was content to offer the responsibilities of my life purpose to anyone remotely interested in taking it. My rational mind was confused, I felt uneasy knowing that I hadn't obtained a university degree. Yet I had studied and had been guided by higher teachers for twenty years. For fifteen years I conducted my own research and found information that continually confirmed the research. I constantly questioned if I was evolved enough to carry the message this book contains. My fears and doubts niggled at me for many years. And yet, I truly believe that we all have an important life purpose, something unique and special, that we all contribute to the world in our own way.

Initially, I channelled information. I was then led to books that confirmed the information I had received was correct. These books depicted esoteric wisdom from ages past, quantum physics, books written by leaders of religion and books channelled by spiritual elders. I also received new information that provided me with a rounded education. And finally, my dream visions allowed me access to sacred knowledge.

In reality I was well prepared, but my faith and trust in my gifts and abilities, needed many more years to evolve.

My visions provided an important key. Future time would expand an opening, destiny would require me to unlock my heart and transcribe my story. It was now time to work with the healer, a man who would offer healing. He would assist me to rediscover and align to the purity of my soul. This would allow me access to my Higher Self. Within my body lay dormant the pain and suffering I had endured from the time of my birth until my fortieth year. I would learn to stop internalising pain. I would learn to open my heart to love. I would learn to look beyond the cruelty other people inflict from their pain bodies and access a greater understanding of their behavioural influences. Finally, I would allow myself and those around me the grace to heal.

As I became more aware of life's problems and tribulations, I would realise that people are scared, mostly confused, needing to understand who they are and the world we live in. We all have so many questions that swirl within our minds, perpetually left unresolved and unanswered. Part of our basic fear is of the new, the untried and the unknown. To change ourselves we need to change our lives. To change our lives we need to access our inner selves and be open hearted to receive the tools to change the way we think. Most importantly of all, we need to understand the mechanics of our pain body. This will create a life that is breathtakingly beautiful, but unimaginable to you just yet!

As I healed further, I accepted a voluntary position at a community centre. Helping others filled the physical void that closing my heart had ensued. This led to public speaking on a variety of topics. Some people visited the centre purely out of curiosity, others attended because they were encouraged by family and friends. During the duration of two hours, they were encouraged to access real life tools that would activate positive change in their lives. We allocate so much of our time during the day to working, caring for family and friends, deploying acts of service and kindness, and often forget to express love and compassion to ourselves.

During the summer of that year I was introduced to a wonderful couple called Sienna and Matt. Their love and respect glistened like jewelled luminous stars; intrigue encouraged me to look deeper. Watching intently, the purity and beauty of their love warmed the shackles of my sensitive heart. Refocusing my attention, I watched as Sienna began to walk around the room. She held her drum in her tiny hands as it reverberated to its own unique rhythm. Two soft doe eyes expressing tender love, and a heart with the strength of a lion and the tenderness of a butterfly stood before me. Was I breathing? Only just. She smiled.

My heart began to sing a melody of tunes, blissfully aware. I felt the love and respect bestowed by this beautiful woman. An intense energy hit my heart as it expanded. I took a slow, deep breath. My heart was open to Divine Union once again. As the drum connected to my heart I felt a deepening sense of peace. A spark flickered, long forgotten. A sacred love buried deep inside was ignited and flamed to access new heights. It was time to heal, to open the secret cavern to Divine Union once again.

The next day I called the healing centre and requested an appointment to see the healer. I was informed that my timing was amazing as Michael had recently returned from Europe and was scheduling healing appointments during the week. I smiled to myself. The events that occur in my life are never a slip of luck or good fortune. They are a carefully orchestrated plan of events directed from a higher source of loving presence that activates the path before me.

With trepidation I approached the healing centre for my appointment. There was a knot in my stomach the size of a small mountain. My hands felt clammy and sticky as I nervously walked up a small flight of stairs. Michael greeted me warmly at the reception desk. He smiled politely, which I half-heartedly returned, and he led the way toward the healing room. I followed him at a distance. He was a man after all I reasoned, convincing myself that I was just being careful.

The room was furnished with two black chairs. A small table and pale blue lamp were situated to the right. Picture frames covered the walls displaying flower prints in pinks and purples. The lighting was softly dimmed. His eyes glowed with intent and purpose as he looked soulfully at me. I was totally unprepared for the compassion they portrayed. What did we have here?

He spoke sparingly, gently, emphasising certain phrases to explain a point of reference and as he did so he leant forward in his chair. I was feeling intimidated and extremely uncomfortable being in such close contact with a man. It had been seven years since my heart lay broken like pieces of splinted glass at my feet. Michael could see that I had been surviving by skimming the surface of life. I was only fooling myself, imagining that I was actually a participant in it. I quickly buried this significant piece of information as irrelevant. The hatred I felt toward men blurred my sense of fairness. On the one hand I knew that my judgemental opinion of Michael was neither fair nor just, yet on the other hand I did exactly that. He was judged and found guilty on all counts for being a man! Poor Michael, there was much work to be done.

My pain resided around the fact that I was scared to love a man again. The morose fear that love would find me once more lingered and I was determined that was never going to happen again. An easy tranquil peace pervaded my life. If I was honest, I would have considered the fact that I was not experiencing or expressing love myself. My intent was focused on teaching other women how to access Divine Union. An important part of my life was missing. The pain I had endured reminded me that I didn't want to experience a broken heart again. However, my inner-self, my Spirit knew better and so the healing began.

After conversing with Michael for fifteen minutes he explained that he was ready to commence the healing. It would consist of placing his hands on the front of my body that connected to centres which oscillated in alignment with certain organs. Eastern mysticism refers to these centres as Chakras. A cold unfriendly smile was reflected on my face. He was going to touch me? I don't think so!

At this point I contemplated suggesting that he must have taken leave of his senses and walking out of the room. As if I was going to let him touch me. Mild panic slid around the area of my lower abdomen. Should I flee or voice my trepidation? Before I could formulate my plan I remembered suddenly, without knowing how, that I was safe with him and if I inhaled small breaths of air slowly into my lungs until I stopped panicking, everything would be fine.

He retreated to the bathroom to wash his hands and I visibly relaxed. The healing table was narrow and looked extremely uncomfortable. Deciding to make the most of a stressful situation, I stopped procrastinating and slid onto it. It wasn't as uncomfortable as I had imagined. It was soft, with deep plump cushioning so I visibly relaxed.

Michael returned and indicated where he needed to place his hands, explaining the process clearly so that I would not become unduly alarmed. He asked me to take five deep breaths and allow myself to relax. My heart slowly stopped racing as I became consciously aware of my breathing. To my surprise relaxing became effortless. Michael commenced by placing the palms of his hands on the soles of my feet. Warmth invaded the area and a feeling of wellness arose as energy travelled from my toes to my head. Within a few moments the sensation of vibration started to oscillate the physical atoms of my body. I felt like I was floating.

The vibration stopped of its own volition. Warm hands circled my ankles while the floating sensation continued. The vibration oscillating my physical atoms continued with vibrant intensity. Once again, with no prior warning, the vibration stopped. Warm hands were then placed upon my knees. The oscillation here was also intense. The energy was creating the sensation of floating in a space of tranquil bliss. Then we hit a pothole.

The energy once again stopped and Michael moved his hands. He began to activate my endocrine system, placing his hands on either side of my hips, pumping energy into my ovaries. I nearly had a coronary. The energy felt warm and soothing and then I felt tears sliding down my face, falling onto the pillow. Years of pain and frustration and the denial of my femininity began to surface in waves of release. I was oblivious to the fact that the release of tears was a healthy response. While dealing with so much adversity I had always had to be strong and defiant so it was difficult for me to feel this degree of sensitivity.

Michael then placed his hands on my lower abdomen. I immediately tensed my body. The healing activated the base and sacral energy centres. He continued to work diligently to release my issues and heal the pain I had buried inside. His objective was to facilitate a healing process that would restore my former self. I had become lost in the pain, the pain that had kept me living in fear. The healing would provide balance, encouraging me to appreciate the true beauty that life has to offer. Michael would offer friendship. I just didn't know that yet.

The activation of each endocrine gland told a story that would express in simplistic, yet profound truth, the depth of pain I had endured during my life. This was the connection to healing my pain body. Each centre is connected to an aspect of the following: childhood, relationships, self-acceptance, how we deal with anger and frustration, emotional blockages and heart connection, how we treat ourselves and others, how we speak our truth, and finally, our connection to the higher loving presence that I speak of.

As Michael placed his hands on my heart centre I consciously felt the pain releasing. Suddenly, an all-pervading feeling of sublime love, the sacred love I have felt since childhood emerged from deep within. Within a few minutes I fell asleep.

Gold light hovers above my physical body and I know that I cannot resist it. Within the light a man stands before me. I recognise him instantly as the same man from my dream visions. His face is lightly tanned, kissed by the touch of the sun. Soft hair glistens in the light's embrace and his smile radiates pureness and love. Honey brown eyes search mine. I am joyous, light and free. Slowly I gravitate toward him. He holds his arms wide open and I step into them. My body glows with bright golden light.

My attention is riveted on him. I move a little closer. Heat begins to appear around my arms, upper back and neck. I touch the surface of my arm. Amazing! My flesh is cool to touch. My breathing deepens. A force outside of us pushes ever so gently. Coloured lights dance before my eyes giving the impression of fairies at play. The feeling of having no control is exhilarating, yet at the same time a little frightening. His breathing deepens; his gaze is intently focused on my lips. The love, a life force of its own, touches my face with the gentleness of a fawn. His breath fans my face. The wonderment of this euphoria projects physical sensation into oblivion. I experience the sensation of intense pressure around my head. All I feel is the presence of the sacred and eternal now. My heart explodes allowing love to permeate every cell. His beautiful face is just centimetres away. At last the tip of his nose brushes the side of mine. Our cells explode in the delight of their union. His lips, the softness of velvet, touch mine. His kiss deepens and I know that I am experiencing and accessing Heaven on Earth, pureness itself. He is intent to invoke this sacred trust between us knowing this connection is meant to be. The vision slowly shimmers until it is gone.

Michael placed his hands on either side of my face, and warmth spread throughout my body. The vibrating energy ceased and I knew the healing was complete. Ever so gently I woke up. Having never participated in a healing session before, I had been very sceptical of people who professed such occurrences. Activating the endocrine system produced a link to health and vitality as its function is to help boost the immune system. This man possessed a gift, this I was sure.

A lengthy conversation with Michael followed and we talked about the painful issues that concerned me. He reclined in his chair, his body language and the pensive look on his face indicated that he was listening.

Finally, I was being heard. It mattered to him that I was in pain. It mattered to him that I was terrified to love again. The numbness started to diminish. In its place resided a ray of hope and the stirrings of peace floated within my heart.

Michael brought the healing session to a close and as he did so he indicated that he performed three healings, explaining that I should be the one to make an appointment when I felt the need to do so. This simple request allowed me to resume responsibility for myself. At that point, there was no time to reflect on the vision I had so willingly participated in. I was still reeling from the shock that I had kissed a man. The velvety softness of his lips still lingered. Discussing it with Michael was out of the question. Divulging the information that I experienced visions was not my usual course of action. I accepted that I had visions to facilitate a process for higher learning which, in turn, allowed me to assist other people.

Divine Union continues to exist! I had lost this precious gift once and could not face the thought of losing it a second time. Perhaps my dream visions would provide the answers I sought. Who was the man with the soft velvety lips and beautiful soulful eyes that created such euphoria in my heart? Slipping into the realm of dream visions was soon to become a heavenly abode.

Heavenly Abode

My life was following a direct path to Divine Union once again. My dream visions would release a wealth of knowledge that circled the cavern of my subconscious awareness. In relation to aspects of love connected to the heart, women lead the way. Men follow unless fear prompts them to step back to emotional distance. Conventional relationships exist in the three lower centres. Traditionally, men reside in the base level of survival and women reside in the third centre of emotions. Connection occurs through the second centre of sexuality. This is the origin of human disconnection. We do not activate the higher chakras. Divine Union allows couples to walk side by side, an equality that maintains our originality and purity. Equality is not born of identity. It is born of love, respect, compassion and understanding. As men and women of this sacred relationship in Divine Union, we are not the same but are complements of the masculine and feminine. The complement enhances the totality of embracing the uniqueness of the other's wholeness, bringing to completion the human form that we shall know as Divine.

A few days had lapsed since my healing session and the euphoria of feeling connected once more to the purity of my soul was exhilarating. I danced to the tune of my own unique rhythm and realised that the lightness I felt was familiar and similar to the blissful existence of divinity I had experienced in my dream visions. For one moment—one heart stopping moment—I relinquished the pain I had accumulated and felt infinite peace in having let go. I let go of pain. I let go of resentment. I let go of the hatred I was still burying in my liver. For those few precious days I knew the truth of living life without the self-made prison my accumulated emotional pain had encased me in. It was freedom, pure and simple.

The exhilaration lasted for four days until I was catapulted headlong back to the painful life reality I knew. The healing had restored balance in my body only temporarily, I had not permanently resolved the issues that had caused the original imbalance. As thoughts of judgement and feelings of deep hatred toward Antonio re-surfaced, my cells stopped oscillating at the optimum level.

Once again I am woken in a dream vision. Smoky mist covers the scenery like a sheer silk blanket. Through the veil of wispy swirling white light I can see the silhouette of a man. The mist clears and I smile in true delight. Soft velvety lips smile at me in recognition and I see it is the man from my visions. Adorning his body is a robe of shimmering gold light. I remember wondering if his robe is like a hospital gown at the back, open and glorious for all to see, relishing the image with cheeky delight. The robe shimmers and becomes sheer. The sight of him catches my breath.

My attention is drawn to him akin to the force of a magnet. I experience an incredible urge to run my hands across his chest which has only a smattering of hair, just enough I reason, to entice a warm tingle from my fingers. The robe opens and I place my hands inside. His body heat warms me, soothing my nerves instantly. His eyes search mine as he explains that he is here to teach me on all levels—the heart, the body, the soul and the mind.

Our first experience holds the promise and nervousness that accompanies the unknown. Quickly, I realise the energy flows from outside of us and then simultaneously surges within. Words became obsolete as his attention focuses on the feelings of touch that accompany this level of soul remembrance. My hands tentatively move across his chest. His muscles are firm, yet yielding to my touch. The experience is exhilarating. As strange as it may seem, I feel no fear, no thought other than knowing this connection between us is meant to be. His smile indicates his approval. I am an apt student, learning quickly.

My hands move down his chest nestling the hair, following its direction until I reach his stomach. He is teaching me to access divine love through touch. He is also teaching me to allow my inner-self access to a higher source of love bridging my body to do so, to experience and to know this higher part of myself. Our souls touch and loop through the portal of time via the subtle body and we experience oneness for just a moment.

My hands then continue to move lightly across his stomach. The sensation is sublime. He inhales gently. His breathing deepens, and sensation becomes a visible energy wanting to be felt, loved, honoured and treasured. Instinctively I open my lips. They seek to touch his, my tongue savouring the taste and texture. I feel his heart open to access this higher love. Unable to contain his curiosity, his soft hands touch the smooth texture of my skin. My cells jump over each other vying for his attention.

I am conscious of the exquisite sensation his touch has ensued, yet I am more aware and curious to know more about our higher connection. Our inner-selves are confidently moving and contracting, and I reel at the complexity of all that I am witnessing. My mind feels his touch. How can this be? His mind is caressing mine and the bliss of the experience startles me. My head pulses akin to the thumping of a headache without pain, once more moving and contracting. Something shifts in the cavern of the right side of my heart. A gurgling sound confirms this to be true. His heart centre is fully open now. It swirls and soars as it entwines with mine. Tenderness in his touch returns and I become aware that his hand is placed on the inside of my thigh.

My sacral centre connected to sexuality and creativity begins to pulse with energy. Every cell in my body is awake and I quickly realise that the core of our connection resides in the deepest recess of the higher heart, the divine heart, not in the sacral centre connected to the human body. To my relief the intensity of our connection moves into the emotions of the third centre.

He explains very gently that he needs to release the energy sexually first, purposefully adamant that a higher understanding will be revealed. He also requests that I trust him implicitly. His teachings will show us how to access the Higher Self while living on the earth. This is imperative to the process of his teachings—showing us how to access the purest and highest level of spirit.

Energy above us circles and pierces the top of my head. The love from above is delicious, purity itself, as it cascades on the wings of a snow white dove. My lungs expand and I find myself inhaling large breaths of air. This settles quickly, as the expansion of my lungs increase, the air that I now breathe is light and breathing becomes effortless. My body feels weightless as if I am no longer held by gravity.

I am aware that he has moved me from the chair and I am lying comfortably on my ebony wrought-iron bed. He softly caresses my back to access my subtle body. The subtle body is the key to accessing the Higher Self. His glorious figure stands beside the bed as kneels before me, looking into my eyes, accessing the entry to the most sacred place within me. I return his gaze content to follow his lead. His eyes are touching me with the tenderness of a kiss. He expresses his masculinity reverently, sourced from the higher aspect of divine love.

Conventional relationships are felt sexually and released through the human orgasm, but the Higher Self is never activated in this lower form. The human orgasm without a higher loving connection is a minute doorway to access a path to procreation, nature's way of ensuring the survival of the next generation.

We search for a partner continually looking for our true complement. During our encounters we may find a wonderful source of human love. We may even find a measure of happiness as we view our lives from the physical body-conscious world in which we live. It is imperative, if you are looking for Divine Union, to awaken the knowledge you have stored within. If you experience deep loving peace in your life and glory in your soul, be assured that you are on the right path. If you are experiencing pain and feelings of separateness or aloneness then your inner-self is trying to awaken you and show you that there is more. Oh, so much more!

He removes his golden robe, sliding next to me on the bed. His arms encircle me in a tender and loving embrace. Our connection is subliminal and pure and I long for his touch. Tingles of pleasure catapult along my spine as his lips open to claim mine and his tongue explores the silkiness of my mouth. His lips leave the safety of mine and begin to wander, a searing trail of kisses are planted along my neck. He then nibbles my ear lobe coaxing my cells to dance. They know the intimate beat of his rhythm and revel in the purity that is ours. I am pulled further toward him. The sensation is exquisite. All the while his hands are caressing my skin. Once again, a white-hot energy pierces my heart. Light fills every space within me. I am floating beyond time and space. I only know that I am love, pure love, expressing the highest divine love with this divine man. He explains that he is going to release the energy of divine love through sexual touch.

I nod my head in agreement. His hair glistens as sunbeams peek into the room. I run my hands across his back feeling the sinews beneath his flesh. His chest nuzzles mine and my heart opens deeper to his. We are activated at the level of heart, soul and mind. It is now time for our bodies to connect.

His fingers seek to find the cavern contained within me. I am ready and waiting for his touch. To my amazement I experience the sensation of him making love to me even though he is still lying beside me on the bed. I reel in disbelief, yet my inner awareness pulls me back and I am encouraged to relax. Sensation claims my attention and I open myself to merge with him. My physical atoms begin to vibrate allowing the purity of this love to surge within us. As I experience the height of a physical peak my heart centre merges with his. In that moment, my soul pulls away from my body, connects with my subtle body and merges with our Higher Self, momentarily I am free.

I am flying, with this new found freedom and inner truth. I can see our celestial higher form shining with brilliance and light. How glorious is this gift that we are opening and exploring at this time. Our knowing and utilising of this information will effectively change us and the world we live in. Divine love bathes me softly. A flow of tears are released as I am awed by the feeling of grace.

He touches my shoulder gently, encouraging me to return. My mind has so much to comprehend. I have so many questions to ask but he indicates that my questions can wait. My mind reels with endless wonderment. I am cradled in his arms as we allow a deeper inner communion of our awakened higher hearts. In this moment, words are obsolete.

All too soon it was time for him to leave. He will return, of this I am sure. There is so much more to learn. A smile hovers around his lips as he retrieves his golden robe and gracefully slips it on. He needs a name, I reason. The Golden Man filters in my mind. He walks softly toward the door. Unexpectedly, he returns and looks into the depths of my eyes. Without warning he kisses me deeply, curling my toes in the process. I really wish he wouldn't do that. It turns my brain to mush for a week!

Healing Heart and Soul

Dreams and the waking veil of reality peek through complex blinds of understanding. Did I question my sanity? Absolutely! My thinking changed as I searched outside my cocoon and soared on wings to find a new world of love and light. My life was once filled with pain, rage, fear and indignation. Now the pain was starting to melt like snow.

I searched for reasons to look beyond Antonio's pain body. Refusing to argue with him, I fostered an attitude of gentleness and support. Fear and dread ceased to exist when he approached me. His soul opened and there to be found was his point of light. He had to have one. We all do. We all originate from the loving energy of this light. Antonio is loved as much as I am.

These concepts were difficult for me to accept in the beginning. Initially, I thought that if I opened my heart and offered forgiveness to Antonio that the abuse I endured meant nothing. During the next period of my life I would learn that in forgiving Antonio I would free myself and end my cycles of pain and suffering. This one act of forgiveness would change our lives, taking me one step closer to activating Heaven on Earth.

Forgiveness—true forgiveness—is the healing balm for our world. It opens the heart and soul, cleansing the mind to higher truths and understanding. My life work is dedicated to helping other people access Divine Union. I consider it a blessing and an honour as I marvel at the beauty of my true life purpose. My greatest fulfilment occurs in helping others facilitate a process for change in their lives. Simply offering tools to help people heal their families toward wholeness, love and joy is important if we are to heal on a global level. But first, I needed to obtain a permanent solution for my own family.

Luca was ready to move forward with his life. Rebellion, he reasoned, was the best course of action. His father had become a perpetual thorn in his side and Luca was adamant that he was going to make his father listen. Force does not move mountains or a father's course of destruction for that matter. Their arguments had become more intense and afterwards the times of silence were deafening. Inevitably, I protected Luca as he nursed his emotional wounds.

Once more the sense of powerlessness crept upon us. Antonio was still creating emotional havoc and no one would listen. Respected by teachers and loved by students alike, Luca's behaviour was deemed to be an unfortunate process of puberty. His acts of defiance screamed his need to be heard, that at last someone would listen. They didn't, and he started college life, allowing music to be the light that soothed his soul.

As the eldest child and son, I was aware that Luca felt the burden of responsibility to me and to his siblings. He had a gentle and compassionate heart and it concerned him greatly that we were not able to resolve the issues we faced as a family. Our family doctor encouraged Luca to see a psychologist. He constantly searched for solutions, needing to know if the problem originated from Antonio or himself. While living with an abusive parent, normalcy becomes blurred and the emotional battlefield confuses truth. The psychologist, a man of integrity and inner harmony, allowed Luca to witness strength and gentleness in a man. Inner peace prevailed and Luca made amazing inroads toward facing his issues.

He finally accepted that the problem belonged to Antonio. Making a conscious decision to live his life fully, Luca pursued meditation and began the search for his true life purpose.

A few months later I returned to the centre to see Michael, confirming an appointment for the second healing session. This time I approached the centre with confidence. The healing had created a real difference in my outlook toward life. As each issue became more evident I tried to acknowledge the lesson it was teaching me. These times were hard for me emotionally and mentally, but more importantly, changing my thoughts was having a dramatic positive effect. I refrained from burying pain and came to understand more fully the basis of resolution, letting go and moving on.

I have always believed it is imperative to start at the beginning so I looked at the issues with my parents and found that I felt love and understanding toward my biological mother Olivia. In my heart, I had always felt that she had abandoned me. I now know that I was fostered as a baby for my protection, a decision based on unconditional love on Olivia's part. It was not a selfish desire to leave me behind.

The day of Olivia's sixtieth birthday brought to my attention the degree of love she felt for me. I bought her a birthday present and watched this woman I barely knew in human terms open a floodgate of emotions. She shed the tears of her grief, crying for all the years lost but not forgotten. I felt the love a mother feels for her child and the devastation she endures when her child is gone. We hugged, releasing the core of our pain and I watched as the confusion lifted. The lesson was resolved and a greater understanding filled us. We were finally at peace. In the pain that had accumulated, the feeling of unworthiness to be loved lived inside me. I had also developed a fear of intimacy, terrified that I would be rejected and left alone.

The healing with Michael would prove to be my saving grace in many ways. His gentle heart was known to me and a deeper sense of knowing connected us. I didn't express my belief in re-incarnation initially, and was surprised when he confirmed this same understanding and knowledge. The healing confirmed a shift in the lower family aspect and we talked about my resolution concerning abandonment. His eyes shone with joy knowing that I had taken the first tentative steps toward healing. Michael indicated that I should make my last appointment when the need arose.

I left the healing centre once more floating on a cloud of bliss. As much as I hated to admit it, an affiliation with Michael had blossomed. But I reasoned that the healing would be finished in a few weeks and he would forget I had ever existed.

Some things in life are just meant to be. A final appointment was scheduled for the following month. Arguments with Antonio occurred less frequently now. The quiet times were also longer in duration. Determinedly, I decided that this charade would no longer affect me. My heart longed for the peace and contentment that had settled in all other areas of my life. Much to my children's dismay I started to sing. This would only happen when I was really happy, when my soul exuded true delight.

During the next few weeks I looked at my issues with Deanna, searching for the core of my pain. Alien blood did not run through my veins, even though my cousins would tell you otherwise. I was different, yes. But I did behave normally when I was awake. It was only when I was asleep that otherworldly influences emerged.

Belated understanding came to the fore when Deanna explained her reasons for wanting to keep me safe. As a young woman Olivia had been attacked by a group of men and my family wanted to protect me. Deanna's childhood had also created deep fear within her and she felt compelled to protect me from the dangers of life. In protecting me from the dangers, I was also denied the growth and responsibility to learn from my own mistakes, and to cultivate the wisdom we obtain.

Through the eyes of an adult, I could see now that my married life with Antonio was going to be intensely painful. The innocence of my visions would allow me to retreat into my own private source of love. It also became obvious to me at this stage that Deanna's tongue lashings were the result of the loss and betrayal she had endured of her beloved Tom. It was her heart that held the key; it was her heart that taught me unconditional love. Her capacity to love, her warm sense of humour and beautiful hugs were like honey nectar, sweet and soothing with just the right amount of oomph. The love she gave to my children as their carer while I worked allowed them the privilege to know first-hand the heart that loves them dearly. All things considered she loved to the best of her ability and we love this way because of her.

I arrived at the healing centre to find Michael waiting to start our third session. The healing of my centres once more confirmed the issues I had resolved. Delving into ourselves, resurfacing pain and finding avenues of resolution is demanding work. Michael was very encouraging and happy that I was progressing so well. We chatted and laughed like life-long friends. It was amazing. Very subtly I was returning to life, finally allowing myself the gift of friendship with a man. I was also grateful for his presence and gentleness. He had literally brought me back to life, showing me simplistically how to live without fear and how to re-discover the joy of living with love.

Our friendship was destined to continue. The co-ordinator of the centre indicated an interest in meeting Michael. She was curious as to the reason for my euphoric state of well-being. He was invited to speak at the centre concerning the healing work he performed. Many people are not aware that such modalities exist, nor the scientific evidence of their success. Because of Michael's warmth and love of humanity, he was accepted immediately and people started to request appointments to see him. Our friendship blossomed. Michael invited me to observe his healing sessions and so my research began.

During the course of this early research, I was profoundly moved as I watched the depth of pain and suffering people endured. Just how do we cope? How do we function? Life can be acutely horrible at times and yet most of us survive. We find a way to go on. We continue with our lives, not particularly happy or fulfilled but believing this to be our lot in life. We are not aware that we deserve more. We are not taught to embrace the light of our true essence, to grace our soul. Some people are not even aware that they have a soul. They only know that they are filled with pain—they live in the shadows of their pain body—and life is just like that. The truth that resides in our inner hearts tells us that a higher source of loving presence guides us. We are so loved. It is our pain body and the accumulated suffering that resides there that shuts out this love. It is we who hide from its light. It is our responsibility, our duty of care to awaken to its glorious embrace and open ourselves to receive.

Antonio watched the steady glow of the metamorphic transformation that appeared before his eyes. He was not sure about my sudden burst of happiness, nor was he pleased with the idea that it might continue. Controlling me was now on his mind. I had decided that when the children reached adulthood there was nothing to keep us connected. My plan was quietly fermenting. It was a waiting game. Our children would reach adulthood and then I was going to leave. Of this fact I was adamant.

Luca's life progressed significantly in his life direction and he found a passion for writing inspired poetry and songs. He has a musical gift and taught himself to play the guitar.

My father played guitar, piano, piano accordion, mouth organ and he sang directly from the heart, always insisting to me that music is the nectar of the soul. Music can heal us if we allow it to do so. He bought my first piano when I was five and taught me how to play, sitting me on his lap with my tiny fingers laid over his. I was taught the brilliance of melody and the necessity of light and shade. The intensity of his joy and delight was infectious and these are the memories I have of the teachings he gave. Our time together was always limited, cramming a lifetime of teaching into it. Somehow, his soul knew that we were living on borrowed time.

Eventually, Luca was employed by the corporate world that he fought so hard to change, and created an immensely positive impact. His passion revolves around the synergy of merging science and spirituality as he pursues Matrix Energetics and various healing technologies. These new energy systems are producing amazing results.

Marc progressed physically in leaps and bounds. He won two soccer league best and fairest awards for his age group. The path of destiny loomed auspiciously in front of him. His skill and expertise, his love and steadfast purpose shone through with great brilliance. However, the destiny path was slow; new opportunities headed toward him in trickles and not in the grand way we had all envisaged.

Issues with his father surfaced which he was unable to resolve. At eighteen Marc faced his father in an act of courage and defiance. He left home. My heart hurt for the loss of my child and for him needing to leave in these uncomfortable circumstances, but soared for his right to freedom.

Three years passed and Marc still harboured anger and resentment toward his father. But due to financial difficulties he was forced to return to live with him and as they resolved their issues, soccer contracts began to emerge. He was recruited by a management team and prepared himself to leave our island state.

Bella has astounded me with her love and many faceted friendships. She became a friend to all, drawing toward her young men and women who needed love and guidance. She possesses an open heart as she focuses her life this way. Her purity and laughter lights up a room and I adore being in her company. Unknowingly, she intimidates her peers at times. Mother Nature has blessed her with many gifts. It is awe inspiring watching someone so young find strength and character of truth and purpose. Emotionally, she is miles ahead and has had lessons of jealousy and resentment to deal with. I am giving her tools of resolution. The outcome is not always immediate but to her credit she is persevering as she progresses steadily.

Lorenzo, my angelic baby matured and started his path toward structured education. He realised very quickly that not everyone was like his mum. Lorenzo has the gift of knowing. He knows if people are telling the truth. The awareness that he is different has troubled him deeply at times, leading to him rebelling against the system, challenging the adults around him, and testing the limits of our patience. His many friends love and support him and his humorous antics provide much needed relief. As he masters this world, I watch, intrigued with his knowledge. His understanding of people and our world is amazing and I wonder if teaching will be his future purpose. He absorbs the lessons of this world and I am grateful that he teaches me something new every day. Much to our delight and amazement he graduated from college and is busy pursuing the next phase of his life. I am sure there will be parties involved!

Michael and I continue our friendship. We worked together for five years witnessing the miraculous that occurs when people open their lives to healing, growth and change. My research expanded so much during this time. Michael is a kind, gentle man who needs to leave the world in a healthier place than he found it. His love of nature blossomed to the point that rare birds find sanctuary in his garden and show their appreciation by spending time there. The study of spiritual subjects is always near and dear to his heart and he constantly strives to be the very best that he can be.

Unfortunately, the physical world beckoned and he returned to retail sales. We shared many magical moments, helping others to awaken and take the necessary steps forward with their lives. The safe haven of friendship we created was idyllic. When Michael returned to sales it was a sharp reminder to me that nothing stays the same, everything changes and evolves. Some people enter our lives for a reason; some people enter for a season. And some, like Michael, enter for a beautiful friendship somewhere in between.

Wings of Love

Life was blossoming for our family in beautiful ways. However, a lesson was hovering just around the corner. The next lesson for us to endure was the finality and loss incurred in death. Death has a way of questioning the totality of life. It has a way of reaching inside and ripping the heart into tiny pieces. The loss of a loved one is palpable. It was my time to experience the loss contained in death first hand.

My beloved mother would pass away with the assistance of angels. She was going to pass into a world of euphoria unimaginable to us, to a realm of love and light where she would encounter the peace of pure bliss. I was just so unprepared to cope with this loss on my own. Was I ready to let her go? Not yet. Her death opened a portal and I acknowledged that reliance had been built as we grew in age and mutual respect. It was time for me to grow up and to accept responsibility. It was time for my mother to leave and for me to take the reins. I just needed to learn how to do that.

In the meanwhile, my nocturnal sensual experiences with the Golden Man continued in my dream visions. The energy of divine love was still venturing into my heart, body, soul and mind. His touch would ignite me like the lapping of fire, provoking the experience of bliss beyond the physical world. It was difficult to function for a few days after our encounters of a pure bliss kind.

During the healing and research sessions with Michael, people would often comment on my child-like innocence and the possibility that I possessed a secret. I would often find Michael looking at me wondering what pervaded the glow around my head. He was too much of a gentleman to ask me what the secret might be, which was fine by me! How could I explain any of this to him? The bliss of the energy I experienced with the Golden Man was incredibly real. Contentment settled upon me in ways I could never have imagined were possible. My Divine Union would enter my life in his own time. My intuition knew that not all the answers I needed were present yet.

I trusted the dream vision experiences implicitly; they were informative, safe even. But trust issues with men were still evolving slowly. Allowing friendship with Michael opened my heart to many possibilities. However, friendship and personal love are two totally different things. Friendship is safe. Michael allowed our friendship to evolve at a safe distance and I always felt protected by him. It was time for me to look at my many unresolved issues concerning men.

Releasing the lessons I learnt with Andre took three years to accomplish. Like layers of an onion they were peeled away one at a time, until I was ready to accept a healthy future relationship. Stitching the splintered shards of my heart was painstakingly endless, like embroidery needlework, delicate and deliberate.

Life lessons wait for no one. As Deanna's health slowly deteriorated I was introduced to the heartache I had envisaged. We knew her heart was weakening. A physical examination by her doctor indicated that her life was quietly diminishing. Deanna had survived a heart attack, two lung operations and a major stroke in twelve years. Her inability to survive this current crisis seemed surreal. Living without her loving presence was unimaginable.

Bella and I visited Deanna on a bright Saturday afternoon. It happened to be the day before she died. She was sitting in her favourite chair watching television. We shared news with her concerning particular family members that she loved to hear about. She had lost her ability to speak as a result of a stroke eight years earlier but her faculties were still as sharp as a tack. The three of us were laughing and giggling like young girls. We kissed her soft weathered cheek and promised to return to see her in a few days. Her twinkling blue eyes held the secrets of mischief and this day was no different.

Sunday morning arrived. Deanna woke unusually early, waiting to be served her toast and cup of tea. This was her morning ritual. But she was restless for most of the day and uncharacteristically quiet. Her restlessness increased and at 3.30 pm she put on her pyjamas and ventured into bed. As 5.00 pm approached it was evident to all that she was dying. Our family doctor was notified and he arrived at 5.30 pm to find Deanna sitting upright in her bed with her favourite pillows plumped up behind her providing support.

It was at this time family members were called. Confusion was paramount with people crying and distraught as they surrounded her bed, adamant they were going to spend those last few precious moments with her. I was at the centre, having been invited to speak, and the room was filled to capacity. We weren't expected to finish until 8.30 pm. My sister Charlotte and a few family members asked for someone to collect me from the centre. No one did. So, I was blissfully unaware of the drama unfolding at home.

At 6.50 pm, the doctor checked Deanna's heart once more and confirmed that death was imminent. She gently closed her eyes and then just as quickly, they fluttered open. Her twinkling eyes were vibrant as she searched the faces and looked at each one. She knew she was going home. This was her personal goodbye, an exchange of the love she felt for her family. Just like a mother hen, she counted her chicks and knew that one was missing. A final breath and then she very peacefully passed away.

At 7.00 pm I began to speak. As I lifted my head I heard a choir of angels begin to sing. To my amazement I saw a white light in the silhouette of woman. Hovering beside her were two beautiful angelic beings. They were singing "my cup runneth over with love". This was the song Deanna used to sing to me as a child. The melody was crisp, clear and blessed with the purest love. So awed by the spectacle before me, I stopped speaking to watch the scene unfold. Curious eyes were focused on me questioning silently as they wondered what was happening. In that moment I knew someone had died but not for one moment did I think it was Deanna.

Unbeknown to me my beloved mother had died and she knew that I was not with her. I was graced with the sight of watching her journey home. Tingles of energy ran up my spine repeatedly as I watched the breathtaking spectacle unfolding before me. As a result of this experience I will never fear the process of death for those whose time it is to die. My prayers and thoughts are for those left behind who have to carry on in the physical world without them.

My sisters, grieving intensely, performed the ritual of washing our mother as a last sign of respect. Two daughters bathed her tenderly, caring for her and talking to her quietly. At last her grey hair was combed. She looked lovely, dignified and rested, her hands placed across her chest in the position of gentle repose.

I returned home from the community centre at 10.00 pm to be told of Deanna's passing. It seemed fitting that I wasn't at her bedside at the time of her death. I knew the wailing would have been intense. Many days later I was told of the time of Deanna's passing. It was then I realised the timing of her death was within minutes of me hearing the choir of angels sing. The visitation was a confirming gift.

My family felt Deanna's presence for days after the funeral and sought direction and guidance to help them cope with their grief. Sometimes, it takes a tragedy for us to open to the truth of this higher loving presence.

Keeping busy is the avenue I pursue when stressed. I returned to the community centre a few days later. A colleague expressed his condolences concerning my loss and as we chatted he explained that he still retained deep grief concerning his mother's death. It was twenty years since his mother had died. To help to release his suppressed emotion, I encouraged him to write a letter to her. Afterwards I thought that perhaps writing a letter to my mother would help me to release my grief as well.

Deanna's funeral was scheduled for Friday morning. My brother Neil requested that I read the letter I had written as the eulogy. Initially I agreed. But on the day of her funeral I was too distraught and declined. Some things in life are destined to be, gifts even, from those who love us dearly. The Reverend attending the service had not been informed of my decision to not read the letter. After listening to the haunting sounds of Ave Maria, she asked me to step forward with the reading I had prepared.

I froze. Before I could decline, Charlotte stood up and made her way to the podium. She turned to me, her heart hurting with grief, and said, "We wouldn't defy our mother when she was alive and we are not going to defy her now, you need to get moving." The presence of my mother's love seemed to envelope me like a comforting blanket. Nervously, I approached the microphone. A gentle peace settled upon me. My legs wobbled like jelly as they held my body upright. I inwardly prayed they would support me until I had finished speaking. With Charlotte by my side, I spoke with clear and heartfelt intent.

A Mother's Love

I write this today as a letter of appreciation and deep gratitude, but also as a valve to release my grief. You will leave us soon. I think I am prepared and accepting that it is time to let you go, but still, I feel it is way too soon. I turn back the clock and I am reminded of the words "A Mother's Love" that special quality instilled in the heart and soul of a woman. Sometimes, if we are really lucky, we will meet a woman who can inspire others to fulfil their dreams and life purpose. You are this woman.

Because formal education was denied to you, your main purpose in life was to help us. You encouraged us to achieve our dreams and wishes, but gave us so much more. You gave us wisdom, pearls of wisdom that have stood the test of time. When you gave me this wisdom as a child I found it to be constricting and annoying. As a mother, I have taken with love and gentleness your special gifts and have used them with a deep knowing in my heart that this wisdom has great truth and honour. I, in turn, have given these gifts to my children because it is important to me that a part of you will still live on in the lives of those you love.

As a child I was overawed by your strength of character. You possess strength, courage, vibrancy and passion for every aspect of life. Your wonderful ability to share the colourful heritage of our family history re-enforced a greater connection for us. Christmas time was filled with the magical smell of cakes baking, pudding and whipped cream, with us children waiting under your feet ready to lick the spoon. Christmas carols filled the air as we felt the tangible presence that something really sacred had happened thousands of years ago. The essence of connection we share for each other as your family is proof of the love you feel for us all.

Your passion for instilling the truth was often released as a tongue lashing. These were legendary and I know I tried hard to please you. As a child I missed the sparkle in your beautiful blue eyes for I was only aware of the essence of right and wrong. As an adult I caught the sparkle in your eyes and I knew you were fostering a deep love to share with us all. As I took those first tentative steps into adulthood I was following my dreams but still wanting to make you proud of me.

As an adult, I realised that I didn't have to try for you had learnt to love unconditionally. In my greatest hour of need your words comforted, supported, uplifted and inspired me to believe in a greater plan beyond myself, and although you could not make my decision for me, you held my heart in your hands for safe-keeping until the break had healed.

You touched the lives of many people, from taking care of their children to offering a kind word of support. I have read that if in one lifetime we can say that we have helped just one person through any form of service, then we have lived a life of distinction. You have accomplished this and so much more. As a family we are very proud of you.

This day will dawn and we will gather together with a heavy heart filled with grief and suffering—each one of us filled with a memory. We will mourn for the loss of the physical you we cannot kiss or touch. We will mourn for the loss of the warmth of your wonderful smile and we will mourn for the loss of the love we have etched in our hearts that we feel is lost. But this is all an illusion. For in reality, you will never leave us. Our mother's love will never die and this is her greatest gift of all.

You will not be here when my sons and daughter have their children. But I know that when I hear them express your pearls of wisdom, I will feel you smile within me and we will KNOW that there is a greater truth to love.

A MOTHER'S LOVE is eternal and that you will be with us always.

We returned to the only family home I have known with heavy hearts, yet determined to celebrate her life. And so we did. Many phone calls were received from people who had attended her funeral, offering their heartfelt condolences, and happy to share wonderful stories and memories with us.

It was here that I realised two important things. Firstly, people were really touched by the letter I had written and had requested permission to use a revised version at their funeral. I was amazed and shocked. Secondly, speaking in front of three hundred people was the kind of daunting task I would usually shy away from. In her wisdom, Deanna knew that I would need to learn to speak with confidence in front of large audiences. It was also imperative that I learn first-hand that my writing touches people's hearts. My life purpose is to impart the wisdom that resides there. Even in death, Deanna was encouraging me to follow my dreams. I love you Mum!

Lonesome Dove

Our families teach us important lessons. They open our heart to love, compassion and tolerance in varying degrees, but most importantly they reflect certain aspects of truth. We have the opportunity to reach inside ourselves to locate the puzzle pieces of life. It is not always easy to see what the lessons are. It is not always easy to understand why the family unit can reflect so many varying degrees of difference. Why are some people born into a family of affluence and others into a state of poverty? Why are some children born healthy and others sick or deformed? Why do babies die? Why are certain adults emotionally stable while others suffer with mental illness?

Throughout my life I have struggled with these questions of inequality. As a teenager I questioned the wrath of a vengeful God, believing in the concept of punishment and then later dismissed that concept. I pondered the theory of random chance, a lucky break, or perhaps the role of the dice. None of these concepts offered any explanations that satisfied my questioning mind. Re-incarnation offers an opportunity for us to consider that we are re-born, to look upon our lives in reflection, to balance the consequences of our actions.

In the quiet times of reflection I also knew that Antonio and I needed to end our marriage so that we could both be free to love again. This life is about creating new beginnings. Resolution is the key. Our lives travel through the inconsistency of intricate twists and turns. The past two years had provided opportunities which created immense inner peace and purpose. I opened up to the beauty of my soul and in doing so; I discovered the beauty to live my life joyously, to find my true life purpose. A special turn of events provided an opening to reach the key of resolution.

The episodes of Antonio's violence had decreased to such a degree that I developed a sense of nonchalance. Days perfectly unfolded like the lapping of ocean waves, they were content and peaceful and evolved without preconceived effort. In addition, I had developed many sweet warm friendships that filled my heart with love.

Because my life purpose involved accessing a direct ascending link to Divine Union once again, it became clear to me that I needed to resolve my issues with Antonio. I couldn't nurture divine love while still legally married to him. There had to be an answer. When I visited a psychologist, I was informed that there were avenues I could pursue concerning Antonio's interference in my life. Truthfully, I was more terrified to leave than to stay. My fear kept me bound in self-inflicted, torturous and uncomfortable pain that always led to more suffering. There were many choices available that I continually chose to ignore. Many times I have been asked the question, "Should I have left my marriage earlier?" The answer is yes. It's important to seek help and protect your emotional fragility and that of your children. I couldn't see a way out then, but now I know that incredible help is available.

I have heard it said that when you hit rock bottom the only way to go is up. I was about to hit this place. Antonio became aware that Michael and I had formulated a strong friendship. He was livid, believing that Michael was the reason for my glowing aura of health. When I told him that our friendship was platonic he looked at me with contempt that conveyed his disbelief. I could see a plan formulating in his mind as the cog wheels began to turn. A sense of panic and dread arose as I sensed his passion for power and dominance surface again. Antonio believed that if his actions became intolerable, Michael, like Andre, would become intimidated.

During an argument two weeks later Antonio demanded that I forego my friendship with Michael. I refused. He fumed for weeks but said nothing allowing me to believe that he was finally accepting my independence. When I spoke to Michael concerning Antonio's anger and frustration he encouraged me to abide by my decision, to take a stand and remain strong, explaining that he would not relinquish our friendship through fear. He was prepared to tackle Antonio head on if the need arose.

A few months later, I returned home one Wednesday afternoon after attending two healing sessions with Michael. After dinner I was rinsing the dishes preparing to wash them when Antonio walked into the dining room and began to scream in the volcanic display of anger that I had become accustomed to. This particular night something inside me snapped and I yelled back at him inflaming his anger tenfold. He ran from the dining room into the kitchen and he hit my chest and then clamped his hands around my neck. Thankfully, the children had gone to bed.

His large thick hands tightened their grip around my neck and I knew that I was in deep trouble. My throat was being crushed and I was struggling to breathe. I tried to squirm out of his grip but his strength in anger was too strong for me to move. It felt as if I had endured the pain for an eternity whereas in actuality only a few seconds had elapsed. Thoughts of dying became a reality and I knew instinctively that I had to protect myself. My hands formed a fist and, with all the energy I could muster, I punched him in the stomach.

Recognition registered on his face and fear and pain were mirrored in his eyes. He realised, for the first time, that he had really hurt me. As if in a daze he let go of my throat and I staggered backward. I ran past him toward the bathroom and locked the door behind me, half expecting him to follow. He didn't. I sat on the edge of the bath for an hour. Coloured bruises were beginning to form around my throat. Dark shadows had also appeared on my chest from the initial strike. At this point I truly questioned whether our struggles would result in my death. It was difficult to imagine a different outcome. Antonio seemed intent on pursuing this path of destruction.

There was a tentative knock on the bathroom door. Antonio whispered that he wanted to talk to me. I declined and asked him to leave me alone. He suggested that I call the police, acknowledging that he deserved to be arrested. Believing that I had nothing left to fear, I unlocked the bathroom door. As I walked away I saw disbelief and so much pain in his eyes. It broke my heart to see us feeling so much hurt and pain.

He accepted that his anger was out of control and that he needed to seek help. No one could ask for this help but him. Something inside him had told him to stop and he sensed that if he had kept the pressure on my throat I would have died. In that moment Antonio gave me his solemn vow and promised he would never hurt me again, and that I was free to live my own life.

The pain in and around my throat was excruciating. For ten days it hurt to swallow. I didn't seek medical attention knowing that I would be asked sensitive questions. Gradually, the bruises disappeared and I slowly regained my strength. The first key had been accessed. And Antonio kept his word. His temper flared, but never to the point that I would fear for my life. The healing I had learnt from Michael would soon be put to good use.

During the five years in which I had conducted research with Michael at the centre, I encountered many warm loving people. One such couple were Pierre and Jane. A few months after meeting Pierre and Jane, Michael invited me to attend a meeting where a group had gathered together hoping to collate chapters for a book anthology. The anthology was to consist of a single chapter of each person's life experiences and the consequent changes that encouraged new growth. The concept was an amazing idea. By that stage, I had written the introduction and first chapter of Heaven on Earth but felt compelled to contribute. My contributing chapter for the book anthology allowed two things to evolve. Firstly, it would help to create a healing catharsis. Secondly, I finally accepted that writing is connected to the growth of my life purpose and that people were deeply touched and positively affected by the message it offered, creating a resonance within their own lives that was shared and understood.

I woke one morning and decided to write the chapter. Once I put my hands on the keyboard, from a still place within, the words begin to formulate. It was as if a tap had opened and streams of descriptive words merged in my mind. A sense of bliss accompanied the narrative and a connection of heart, body, soul and mind revealed its course. Two days later a chapter emerged.

My greatest fear stepped into reality. Other people were being afforded the opportunity to know the real inner me. We agreed to support each other in the process of writing and scheduled a meeting time on Monday evening. It was decided that we would read excerpts from our chapters as a way of sharing our ideas and personal journeys. I was content to allow others to lead the way in sharing their experiences first. I adore stories. This is why I love people so much. We all have a story to share that is interesting and unique, worthy to be heard. It helps us to define who we really are and assists us to know that we can write new stories of change and growth anytime. As I listened intently to the stories, I noted that they were filled with rich vibrant colours of life experiences and wisdom. I loved them all. My heart warmed watching the group members share the most secret aspects of their lives, knowing that acceptance and understanding were prevalent. Judgement was left hanging outside the door. We were so enriched by the experience of honestly being heard. It was a gift. And then it was my turn to speak.

I took a deep breath and allowed the words I had written to speak to those present in the room, not daring to look at anyone until I had finished. However, within a few minutes I could hear giggles as the story progressed. Ten minutes later I averted my eyes from the last page to be greeted by smiles and favourable comments that acknowledged their acceptance of me. For weeks afterwards I smiled with confidence, knowing that I had stepped out of my comfort zone to feel happiness, joy and peace. The encouragement convinced me to continue to help those who seek to heal and move forward to a better life.

Hidden within the story I had written was the blessing of a miracle. I had placed a copy of the anthology chapter on the dining room table. After attending a late afternoon meditation class I returned home later that evening and noticed that the sides of the pages had been turned and a coffee stain was evident on the right hand side. During the afternoon, Antonio had arrived to collect Lorenzo. Antonio had read the story. Now I was nervous. More importantly, was I in trouble?

The book chapter was a condensed version of Heaven on Earth. I had every reason to feel very, very nervous. Antonio walked into the kitchen the following morning. I wasn't conscious that I was holding my breath at first. He gruffly explained that he had read my story and as he spoke he was looking at me very strangely. His facial expression conveyed the truth. On reading my story he had stopped fearing long enough to register that I existed at the end of his temper and anger. Finally, he understood how sad my life had been as he felt the depth of the pain and suffering I had endured. And then he did something totally unexpected.

He asked me for a healing. The story had moved him so much that he located his pain body and asked for help. He wanted me to conduct a healing for him. I nearly collapsed on the floor!

Firstly, Antonio didn't believe in anything he couldn't touch with his five senses. Secondly, he had initially believed that I was the one with the problem. Thirdly, I would have to touch the centres on his body. Oh no! I hadn't touched his body in a long, long time. More importantly, I was being offered an amazing opportunity to restore harmony to his life, to my life and to our family's lives. I accepted it with both hands while profusely thanking anyone who cared to listen.

I arranged the healing session for the following week. It was imperative to do this at home as I knew we would need complete privacy. I was also aware that he couldn't keep still for more than one minute, so I borrowed Bella's portable disc player and arranged soothing music to pipe through the small black ear phones to distract him while the healing progressed.

He removed his shoes and lay on Bella's bed. He placed the earphones on his head and I took a deep breath. I placed my hands on the soles of his feet. He was moving restlessly while fidgeting with the volume on the control panel of the disc player. I ignored his childish attempt of distraction and as I moved toward his centres he visibly relaxed.

On reaching the centre of family childhood the vibration became intense. I sensed and felt his fear and the anger he felt toward his mother. It was that anger he had repeatedly released on me. As a baby his mother had left him in his cot at home alone while she went shopping. He was also left home alone while she worked the afternoon shift at a city restaurant until his father returned later in the evening. As a teenager his mother yelled at him to go out, accusing him that he was always making a mess. He stayed with friends hoping to feel the warmth of family life while avoiding the distance of her heart. His centre rocked in vibration and I watched as he quietly let the pain slip away, knowing that he was now safe.

I put my hand on his heart and activated this centre so that he could let go of hurt and transfer love into the situation, and said, "You cannot change the past only learn from its wisdom. To set yourself free you need to forgive your mother and father."

Antonio's mother Maria was born in Italy. She is the eldest of five children who lived in the blitz of a war zone during World War Two with bombs deploying all around them. When her family escaped to our island paradise they left with the clothes they were wearing. Maria's father treated her differently to his three biological children. He forced her to leave school at fourteen to enter the workforce to financially support her family.

Alberto, Antonio's father, was born in Yugoslavia, the youngest of nine children. Many of his brothers were killed in the Second World War. He left home to follow his dream of freedom and found the sanctuary of paradise soon after. Alberto found Maria when she was nineteen and they married soon after. She vowed to work hard and give birth to one child and provide her child with all the material trappings that money could buy. She considered this a sign of respect in nurturing a child, believing that prestige and social position in life are imperative in order to gain respect.

The vibration ended and I moved my hands to the centre of family and sexuality. The energy here was just as intense as the first. I could feel Antonio's suppressed emotion, his inability to tell me in words the depth of love he felt. His emotions continually frustrated him, there was no safe haven for him to express or release them. He could not admit that he was safe with me. Every time he looked at my face he saw his mother. This fostered the determination that I would never leave him. Sensing the intensity of love that he felt for our children made me smile with joy. This emotion was also buried inside him with no outlet of expression. He loved so deeply, but that love was buried deep in the layers of his pain-filled heart.

Once again I put my hand on his heart. "We cannot change the past only learn from its wisdom." I spoke to him of my sadness and asked him to forgive me for the degree of pain my relationship with Andre had caused him. As the years unfolded in our marriage I had stopped believing that Antonio loved me. My heart longed to express the tenderness of affection and joyous elation in expressing love but Antonio could not share his heart with me, he only wanted to express love sexually, which I could not open myself to. Without expressed love I am not sexually available. Once more the energy ceased.

His third and fourth centres of emotion and heart chakras buzzed with similar intensity. I visibly relaxed. This action opened my heart toward him. In that moment, I did not see him as my husband who had treated me with cruelty. Instead, I saw a broken man who was struggling to understand his life, a little boy terrified of the dark, scared to be left alone. I saw a man who loved his wife and children with honesty but whose pain overshadowed this love, and a son whose burden in shaming his parents created disharmony in his heart. I saw an empty shell of a man unable to connect to his real self. But the most glorious part was his pure point of light, a beacon that shone forth from within the darkness. He could feel his Spirit, his Higher Self and I knew in that moment that he truly loved us all. Radiating in the all-encompassing darkness was a pure white ray of love. It is the connection to the source of the higher loving presence that I speak of. It is the real us. It was the real Antonio. I marvelled at the purity of him, his Higher Self was pure and clean as white snow.

Two silent tears slipped down my face. They were not tears of sadness but of awe. He stopped fidgeting and lay quietly on the bed. A deep sigh echoed from a sacred place within him. He was marvelling at the feeling of connection he felt to his Higher Self, startled but happy to enjoy the bliss, after enduring disconnection for so long. Now I truly understand love.

I moved my hands and placed them on his head. A vibration clear and strong oscillated his physical atoms and they danced beneath my fingers.

The tingles of delight made me smile. A glow of radiating love and peace settled gently upon his face. I knew he could feel his higher connection and I also knew that he was going to move forward with his life.

At last the energy ceased and the healing was complete. He lay on the bed for a few minutes and slowly opened his eyes. The black hue was replaced with a soft brown twinkle. He smiled at me, a real smile of appreciation. We were free of our continuing prison and there was much to smile about. When he spoke there was a gentle resonance in the tone of his voice. He thanked me genuinely for helping him. I accepted his thanks while explaining that I was the instrument and suggested that he should continue quietly with his day. The healing oscillates our physical atoms and the euphoric sensation can cause lightness in the head.

Antonio confirmed that he felt a buzzing sensation in his body for a few days. Confidence and vigour for life had been missing since he was a child and the difference in his manner and speech was metamorphic. He told me that he respected my ability to genuinely offer help to others in the work I now do. The children shook their heads in amazement as they watched their father radiate a happier glow toward them, toward me and toward life in general. Life can be full of such miracles!

Following Dreams

Daylight dawned as dew drops sat languorously lapping the warmth of the sun. Intimacy reveals its own jewelled sensuality. I know the original source of my being and as I heal I am learning to experience its full potential. Always there is more to learn. Always there is more to experience. And as always, I open myself to the purity of divine love. The teaching of Divine Union in its purest form needs to be experienced as truth. I acknowledged at times that I was content to learn the path to access it through the experience of dream visions. The closeness in heart, body, mind and soul revealed a reverent acceptance. My mind was not yet completely comfortable accepting Divine Union in my physical life, there was still an issue in my subconscious that needed to be healed.

The area of subconscious sabotaging had been discussed in various consultations during the previous year. Subconscious patterns of fear were evident, existing in forms of hidden inner conflict that needed to be released and healed. It was relatively easy to accept the conscious aspects that created my pain. Childhood, family and relationship issues were cases of structured events that had occurred. Resolving these issues had been difficult to say the least but the understanding was evident and once I recognised this fact a shift occurred.

My dream visions became more intense and dynamic as I began to feel the Golden Man's presence around my heart physically during the day. My Divine Union would not venture into my life until I had uncovered the reason for subconscious sabotaging. How long would this take? No longer did I feel pressured by time as I learnt to access the now. The dream visions always provided a clue.

My dream vision experiences expanded my knowing and understanding of Divine Union. My husband was destined to arrive in a future time. Andre's love proved to be the tip of Divine Union's existence. He was always meant to leave, thus opening the portal to this higher love.

Men partake of a relationship in speedy pursuit. If a man is interested in you he will call you. If he doesn't call then he is just not that into you. This is not a personal character flaw on his part nor should it be considered rejection on yours. It is just the truth. Rather than tell us this snippet of information men would rather walk across hot coals. Men are also aware that they have difficulty in saying no to a woman, anticipating that she will inevitably react from her third centre of emotions. Men react from the base centre of survival so it is instinctive that a man pursues a woman. This is not a character flaw either. It stems from an evolutionary process. The centres function this way and have done so for thousands of years.

The dance of divine love is depicted as a connection through the eyes. The eyes are the mirror of the soul. If a man is busy looking at your breasts or the shape of your legs or the curve of your bottom then he is not interested in divine love. He is reacting to you from his base centre of lust. If he cannot take his eyes away from yours then he is a divine man operating from his higher heart centre of true love.

The Golden Man returned to teach me and allow me to experience the higher connection of Divine Union. Our experiences were developing in subliminal ways. The sensation of body tingles was now familiar. I quietly reflected for a moment as I prepared to receive his touch. This session occurred to teach me about the deeper mysteries of Divine Union.

A gentle hand activates energy through my body warming my heart. It is interesting to observe that my actions in touching him are instinctive, a remembrance of times long ago. I am activated through my heart, body, soul and mind. Bliss begins to fill my heart and I am conscious that we are preparing to connect through the subtle body to access our Higher Self.

As he opens the pearl buttons on my silk shirt, his fingers brush against my skin. His touch is exquisite. My oscillating atoms begin to dance in tune with the tips of his fingers as they magically entice a reaction. Each time we touch it is with renewed energy as if our eyes, lips and hands are discovering each other for the first time. I am always amazed by this.

His kisses flutter like butterfly wings across my breasts and down my tummy. I inhale deeply, savouring the delight. The euphoria is sweet, sweeter than the taste of nectar. His smile broadens; he is delighted by the touch of my skin.

His mind intimately caresses mine as the room begins to spin ever so lightly. Magnetic energy pulls him toward me. Soft velvety lips explore my mouth as his tongue moves in unison with my heart. I openly expand to allow more delight to encircle me. For just one moment, heat rages in his groin and then flames as it bursts in his higher heart centre. This settles and then pleasure moves from our sexual centres and flames in our hearts. Touching my mind with his thoughts, he urges me to open fully to the wonderment of our experience. It is once again difficult to breathe until a heightened awareness becomes evident. Quickly, my breathing returns to a tolerable level.

His sexuality, now intensely alive, is fully participating in the euphoria of heart, body, soul and mind. A loop of energy connects us as we prepare to experience oneness. Divine love resides in his heart. I stop feeling my own pleasure momentarily and as I do so I begin to feel the depth of the pleasure he is feeling. Somehow we have created the energy of infinity, the sign of the number eight. We are not two but one interconnecting tube. There are no words to describe what this feels like. We are connected in complete unison. Where does he start, where do I end? I just can't tell. Divine Union is circulating a merging between us and the effect is electrifying.

His mounting pressure of pleasure became mine and I know that he is about to experience an intense peak. I also know that I am going to experience this with him. I watch in awe as our divine connection mounts in increments until that sacred moment occurs. We reach the bliss of the sexual peak and his heart surges through me to embrace oneness on all levels. I enter into the aspect of his being and watch as we fly on wings to soar into the divine. The physical release has created an opening of pureness to access our Higher Self; we have experienced the Divine loving presence first hand.

Golden light permeates my base centre. He explains that it is time for me to anchor the golden energy into the physical world. I am amazed to realise that I can now tolerate this higher degree of golden light in my physical body. Love's warmth pours into me though this portal and I gasp with the intensity of it. He smiles and his eyes glitter with cheeky delight. The heat of golden love then pours into my sacral centre of sexuality and creativity. The sacredness of oneness, expressing itself within sexual love expands its light throughout my abdomen. Before I can catch my breath the same heat pierces my solar plexus centre of emotions showing me the depth and reason to bring purity into balance with our feelings. My lower body begins to vibrate with a pure connection to who I truly am.

As each centre activates, it passes to the next a viable energy, a higher life awareness that we do not normally function in. Each centre, feeling the purity of divine love activates the next, and through this I am shown the simplicity, yet complexity of how everything fits together. Each link initially seems separate yet it is intricately linked to all. The power of the link is the higher loving presence that I speak of.

My heart is pierced with the heat of his expression of love. It isn't awe. It isn't euphoria. It isn't bliss. It is pure love. I would describe the experience as deeper than the love you feel when you hold your baby in your arms for the first time, more expansive than watching the grace of a sunrise or sunset, more connected than being immersed in nature. It is the absoluteness of pure love expressed and experienced. The energy stops and I realise the heat of love has completed its journey for now. We look into the depths of each other's eyes. His smile, glorious and ever so beautiful warms me to the depths of my soul.

He closes the pearl buttons on my silk shirt, smiling as he does so. His smile is filled with the radiance of truth and knowing. He indicates that this demonstration is more insightful and profound than any explanation could ever be! His wisdom speaks of profound honesty.

Once again it's time for him to go, he will return of this I am sure. There is still so much more to learn.

The Heart Is Reborn

They say that love is the healer of all wounds. Its tenderness seeps across the thread connected to life and we watch mesmerised as the stitching pulls the edges of the heart together, comforted by the quilt of peace. A tiny flutter is acknowledged. The heart, in the act of knowing, remembers. Sometimes we forget the power of love's healing grace. We forget the treasure of its existence. We acknowledge pain, we acknowledge suffering and we acknowledge hurting so much that we feel our hearts will break. Then we remember. We remember the wisdom that now pervades our being. We remember the joy of love and life's simple pleasures. We remember why we open ourselves—to receive the purity of love's existence in our lives as we bear witness to the miracles that perfectly unfold.

Divine Union reaches out in friendship to those who are open to her loving embrace. It is akin to opening the windows of an abandoned house that is filled with dust, grime and the smell of stale damp air. She watches the transformation as clean pure air circulates through the rooms. The whisper of delight can be heard as the layers of dust and grime are removed and a sparkling clean glow of radiance sits within. She takes a deep breath and she smiles knowing the heart is reborn.

A plan began to formulate in my mind. Antonio needed to feel the euphoria of love again. It was imperative for him to know love without pain, to know the sacred link that is experienced with another person. He deserved to be loved in such a beautiful way. We all do. His future partner had the same thoughts and with the cleansing of his heart she found her way into his life.

Antonio's life quietly unfolded. It wasn't fulfilling or exciting, but he had found peace within himself. He presumed that he would live the rest of his life alone. His care and affection toward us was gentle and nurturing. Luca and Marc were still amazed by his transformation, revelling in their newfound emotional freedom. As a family we were aware that it was time for Antonio's life to evolve. His soul was aware of a higher plan formulating from a distance.

Monica swirled into Antonio's life like a breath of fresh air. She walked into the rambling house of his heart. His emotional window had been shut for many years, with dust and grime laden thickly on its encasement. I watched in amazement as he restored his life until it was clean and sparkling. His eyes shone with renewed delight. The euphoria he felt was startling. We were absolutely delighted for him. In glowing terms he would speak of her gentleness, honesty and integrity. Warmth and goodness encircled her life. She was the mirror image of him in manner, values, ideals and humour.

Antonio found the early days of their courtship stressful. His fear of rejection and abandonment surfaced. Very quickly he learnt that Monica had amazing strength and courage as she taught him the value of problem resolution. The jubilation he felt was contagious and we experienced amazing instances where we witnessed this once extremely unhappy man who had been prone to violent outbursts, blossom into a happier person and a good friend to me. It is difficult at times to express in words the degree of idyllic peace that descended upon us.

Their courtship blossomed and Antonio grew in maturity as he learnt to help Monica restructure her farm properties. He found stability in his masculinity while helping to support her. The discovery of peace was acknowledged for the first time in his life. Shadows of the past no longer haunted him, and the fear of being left alone gradually scattered like ashes in the wind. He started to leave the past behind.

Christmas Day 2004 dawned fresh and crisp. The lace curtains veiled a brilliant blue sky. I busily prepared the traditional lunch that had been such an integral part of my childhood. The aroma was delightful and I sang along with the carols that were playing on the radio. The tangible essence of love was in the room of our traditional family kitchen and dining room that had on so many previous occasions been an arena of fear and pain. I smiled inwardly and outwardly at the beauty of transformation. Deanna's presence was tangible. I know she would be pleased that we had made such amazing progress.

Lunch was prepared with ease and confidence. Now, as a mother in charge of my own family I was carrying on the tradition of cooking lunch as I had been taught, knowing the value of service given to those we love. I pondered that soon enough in a future time, my grandchildren would be born and the magic would increase tenfold. With that thought I heard my mother whisper softly in my ear, "Be careful what you wish for. Your grandchildren will be born when they are ready and if you don't stop daydreaming the potatoes will burn." Some things never change and thankfully our loved ones are always near and close to our heart.

The potatoes were rescued just in time and lunch was served on a table adorned with crystal glasses, fine bone china and the silver cutlery that was only used for special occasions. Antonio joined our lunch celebration and to the amazement of the children he took his place at the head of the table. I observed the scene, grinning as Luca and Marc drank a glass of beer with their father. Bella and Lorenzo sipped on lemonade, watching the scene unfold. A photograph of that special moment was taken inside my heart and was filed away in a permanent place alongside images of the birth of my children. As small children there was only one wish they had at Christmas time. It was to have a family lunch without the fear of violence and disruption that always accompanied special events. The material gifts that had been put beneath the tree paled into insignificance as the true gift of a miracle emerged.

The sound of talking and laughter filled the delicate space in between the delight of their wish fulfilled, and they finished their lunch content not only from the sustenance of food, but their hearts and souls had been nourished by Antonio's acceptance and display of love for us all. There was still more healing to do, but paths had been cleared to ease into a happier life.

Later that afternoon Antonio said farewell. He had made plans to share Christmas dinner with Monica. Once the children had said goodbye they rushed into the kitchen, the four of them speaking at once. I watched as each one spoke in turn, expressing the sheer elation they felt at having their father sitting peacefully in our midst. A proper family lunch, with no drama, no pain. It was deemed the best Christmas ever!

Within the natural occurrence of a relationship the heart opens and a realisation dawns. This dawning happened to Antonio. It was time to take his relationship to the next level. Monica asked Antonio to live with her. Initially, he panicked and then common sense prevailed. He wanted to spend the rest of his life with her, content to grow old gracefully together.

Antonio and I had resolved many of our issues. This was mostly due to the healing and insightful avenues I pursued in my discoveries. Monica was a little intimidated as I lovingly accepted her into our family. I knew they were meant to be together. Eventually we opened up to the gift of friendship. Antonio would look at me suspiciously as well, waiting for me to reveal a hidden agenda but he too, after a period of time, relaxed. I did not change my caring attitude toward his new partner. Our children grew to love Monica as well. In reciprocation, her family opened their hearts to us.

I am aware that we are not our pain and we are not our anger or frustration. We are spirit of infinite magnificence, but mostly we are unaware of who we really are. Genuinely happy that love was flourishing in the hearts of Antonio and Monica, now I was able to start preparing for my own Divine Union to enter my life.

True to his word Antonio continued to help me raise our children, especially playing an active role in Lorenzo's life. He and Monica introduced to Lorenzo the values of country life, and the glory of the land. A keen bushwalker, Lorenzo loved the abundance of nature and they spent weekends exploring the majesty of the land, and playing with the horses and donkeys. In the country, Lorenzo was in his element, with the blood of our ancestors echoing their whispers in his ears. This opportunity has allowed him to experience his heritage first hand.

Lorenzo was of the generation born to heal the past. The restoration of our heritage lay upon our shoulders not as a burden, but as a challenge for us to grow as we matured in our life purpose. His birth, while initially painful for all of us, was the bridge, the way forward that opened the door to the future. The wisdom he shares is evident for all to see. He is a divine child given to us as a gift.

Life is filled with unforeseeable lessons to learn. Once the lesson is learnt we acquire knowledge. To knowledge there is born wisdom. Now possessing wisdom, we know to refrain from making the same mistakes repeatedly. But are you brave enough to learn the lesson and break away from old patterns? With the freedom to decide an alternative way to grow, we open our lives to opportunities that provide an access to the purity of a higher love's presence. If we use our free will to follow the path of lessons, the same lessons will manifest repeatedly until we learn to make informed choices. No one can choose for us. No one else can change our lives.

To implement change is our decision entirely. I could have chosen to keep my role of victim. Antonio could have chosen to keep his role of aggressor. Luca, Marc, Bella and Lorenzo could have chosen not to forgive us and withdrawn from family life. Life is not given to us with a road map or a compass. Living with the glory of this higher love reduces the duration and intensity of pain and confusion. As we open up to this higher love we discover that we truly are never alone. It is our fear that keeps us from discovering this love first hand. Embrace your fears, resolve your issues and dare to believe. It is real!

Our lives progressed with tranquil love and blessings but still there remained an unresolved issue that needed attending to. Antonio's dad Alberto died. I firmly believe the gift of healing changed our lives. During this time Antonio felt real pain—heart-gripping pain that accompanies the loss of a loved one. During the months of intense pain he grieved until finally the pain subsided, and he realised that his mother needed his strength for the first time in her life. Antonio became her guiding light and tower of strength. The showdown was ready to begin.

The capacity of human knowing is astounding. Before Alberto passed away he made peace with me. He kissed the children and spoke to Antonio concerning details of importance two months prior to his death. The children adored their grandfather. He taught them, in his way, about life. His chuckle was delightful and his passion for life was evident in all that he did. Bella was the twinkle in his eye. From the time she first started to walk she would follow him everywhere. He was affectionate, cute and cuddly, her very own living teddy bear. He lavished her with his time and affection and she has the wisdom of having experienced gentle love from two of the most important men in her life. His gift of love she will take with her on her journey into womanhood as she accesses the same gentleness that is within her.

Maria coped with Alberto's death in the way that was natural to her instinct. Denial! She denied that he had passed away. Her venom circumnavigated her heart until the pain had nowhere else to go. It exploded and I was the recipient. During a phone conversation that started like any other, her hostility reached boiling point. She blamed me for Alberto's death. Finally, I snapped. The abuse had been happening for too long. It was important to give sympathy and I was sympathetic for her loss but in the recess of my mind I knew this was the perfect opportunity for us to resolve our issues once and for all.

I allowed her accusations to reach a tirade as the anger buried deep inside her overflowed. Tired of carrying so much pain, she was exhausted. For the first time in twenty-one years I allowed my own pain to be released from its storage and I finally told her how I felt. Energy reeled its way up my spine and I spoke with authority, not with bitterness or hatred. She demanded that I accept her evaluation that my life was worthless, that I was a disgrace. I refused. My life had found meaning and purpose. Sadly, she was not a part of it; she had not wanted to know me. The only truth she could see was that I had taken her son away from her. But this was not love, it was control. She would never accept my right to love my husband. Her hatred and bitterness kept our lives separate.

Half an hour later the conversation ended. She apologised, agreeing that her painful loss was debilitating. I offered sympathy but refused to be bullied by her anymore. We agreed to respect each other and a new door opened. Resolution had occurred. As I placed the telephone on the handset I felt such a sense of relief.

My greatest fear had been faced and dealt with head on and my heart soared with accomplishment. Resolution does not mean seeing the same point of view; it means honouring the truth of the other and not holding on to resentment or pain. We agreed to treat each other with respect, believing that each of us had the right to sit with the truth that is ours.

During the next two years Maria was told that Antonio was having a relationship with Monica. We sustained our truce during this time and I would converse honestly with her concerning my life with Antonio. Often, she would change the topic of conversation and I accepted her view of avoidance. I knew the truth. I had lived it. The truth was too painful for Maria to accept, it was much easier to pretend that it had never happened.

Gradually Maria became accustomed to the gentleness of my nature. She understood that I facilitated programmes to assist people in enriching their lives. One day Maria decided to set a trap for Antonio. She waited patiently for six months for him to tell her of his relationship with Monica. Month after month she asked him if he had anything to tell her. He indicated that there was nothing new happening in his life. Antonio was scared. He refused to tell her; frightened that Monica would leave their relationship if she met his mother.

Finally, the erupting volcano exploded. When he visited her home one day, Maria screamed her disappointment at Antonio. The one fear he still held within his heart surfaced. His mother told him that she knew he had hurt us and demanded an explanation. Finally, Maria asked him to leave her home and not return until he was prepared to tell her the truth.

On a cold mid-winter afternoon I received a telephone call from Maria. She was upset and began to speak softly. Finally, the dam of her emotions broke and she spoke the words I had waited twenty-three years to hear. She accepted that I had not stolen her money and that I had raised the children admirably on my own. At this stage in my life I had no need of an apology. Forgiveness, compassion and the understanding of the life lesson had occurred for me many years earlier. However, I was aware that an incredible weight had lifted from her shoulders and this was heart-warming to witness.

The children continue to love Maria as I do. We accept her way of thinking as her own. She has mellowed now, wanting to spend the rest of her life peacefully, and hoping to see her first great-grandchild. Maria is yet to meet Monica. I have volunteered to mediate in helping them to resolve this one last issue. Antonio and Monica have future plans to marry. When they return, a party has been planned where both families will celebrate and enjoy each other's company. Together, we will all celebrate their wedding.

Freedom from the Past

The elixir of love was talked about during my formative years. The topic of sex, however, was taboo. My mother did not discuss it, yet I saw, heard and felt it all around me. Adults whispered of its existence in hushed tones. No one bothered to explain to me that it could be experienced in its pure form as an integral part of divine love. Our sexuality, when expressed in its exalted form contains the seed of our being. Divine Union heals and leads us toward the connection of heart, body, soul and mind, gaining access to a purity of love we have forgotten. The awakening is the beginning of a new way to live and a new way to express the truth in essence of who we really are. Now is the time of remembrance, a time to re-connect the sacred expression of the feminine and masculine principles.

Warm hands projecting white-hot heat touch my arms and I am woken in a dream vision to find bliss radiating in my heart. The now familiar heat pierces my centres one at a time. I am dreaming in a tranquil pool of love. A sense of deepening peace surrounds me. Divine Union is subliminal, all encompassing, as I remember what it feels like to be connected on all levels.

My health and vitality had improved dramatically and the love I felt toward others was boundless. This feeling was accentuated because of the depth of love I now felt for myself. We are all integral parts of an implicit whole. My existence, like yours, is the glue that keeps life intricately linked together. We reside as brothers and sisters creating pathways toward a potential magnificent life.

I stretch my muscles as delicious energy swirls within and around me. I am conscious of the exquisite sensation his touch has ensued. A hand emitting heat is placed upon my waist. The vibrations are gentle at first, and then they begin to ripple in intensity. His delightful chuckle accompanies a sweet kiss placed upon my cheek. Intrigue lingers as I observe him, his subtle body is the colour of spun gold. Exhaling deeply, I know that I will need to expand my lungs to their optimum level to breathe.

The intensity of his touch ignites my atoms like the lapping of fire and I gasp for breath. The heat we generate is nearly unbearable. His voice, soothing and calm, asks me to breathe slowly and steadily. I feel honoured and so loved. Heat encircles me entirely, and bliss fills me to the brim. He asks me to relax as there is more for me to experience.

My breathing returns to normal. The heat, circulating with intensity is filling my abdomen. I am light and free. My base, sacral and solar plexus are activated and a spinning vortex of light surrounds me.

My heart centre opens to access the conscious reality of my higher heart and it is pierced with the heat of his love. The sense of contraction now pulls energy into a different spiral of light. The sound of his voice, soothing and sweet indicates that the path to knowing is obtained from the wisdom we gain through our experiences. His wisdom speaks directly to my heart. My throat centre vibrates and I have the knowing that I facilitate a higher will in allowing myself to open up to the experiences of divine love. This centre is humming a clear pure melody.

White light pierces the brow and crown centres in my head. My pituitary and pineal glands contract purposefully. The feeling of pure love fills my head and I think that I may faint with the intensity. He is encouraging me to enter fully into the glory of his being, touching and filling my soul with his love until I can expand no further. Without warning, I acknowledge an explosion in my head.

His warm body moves closer, his loving arms hold me in a tender embrace. His eyes twinkle as they look into mine. His lips brush against my cheek, and tenderly his hands intimately caress my skin. A rhythmic motion sweeps us in unison as my body opens fully to accept his. I rejoice in our connection as he continues to permeate my body and soul.

The magnetic energy of pressure increases, my atoms now oscillate at an accelerated rate. My cells gravitate to the subliminal energy of his presence. I am experiencing the contracting of my cells and they dance once more to the beat of his unique drum. He is connected to my heart, my body, my soul and my mind. He now encourages me to release the energy cascading through us, and to allow our bodies to open fully to the divine together.

Bubbles of orgasmic release peak and then begin to circulate in my lower abdomen. The energy then pushes my soul, connects my subtle body and then loops through my heart centre toward our Higher Self. I watch it soar to completion. Light gently fuses in my head. To my amazement we are free; we have merged soul and spirit. I witness us swirling, entwined perfectly as one. We are free momentarily from the constraints of the body and have connected through the soul to pure Spirit. Love permeates every aspect of every cell. I hear the faint sound of a voice that murmurs, "Wait for me. I will find you soon."

After this experience, I felt so different. I am different. I was also ready to face the completion of my life purpose and bring to life the glory of the love I had just experienced.

There was acceptance and understanding that I was fully healed and ready to experience Divine Union once again. I had so much to look forward to. A man of gentleness, integrity, and infinite love would find me now that I had tenderly mended the shattered fragments of my human heart.

I had been shown the value of experience as we learn to grow in love and acceptance. I now knew love. I now knew wholeness. One day I would know completion. The complement of my higher heart, my Divine Union would open a doorway for us to find each other and I would experience the love that is my birthright.

A deep sleepiness overcame my senses. Snuggling under my doona, I savoured the glory of my experience. Closing my eyes momentarily, I decided to relax for a few moments.

The energy of a dream vision pulls my awareness into view. I see myself swimming in an ocean of tranquil blue water as I witness an arm with a long beautiful hand reach down and pull me bodily out of the water. I take a deep breath of air and to my amazement I know the hand is symbolic, a representation of our higher source of loving presence. I am lovingly placed on the top of a mountain with a very high peak. At the summit of this peak the most glorious blinding white light pierces my crown centre through the top of my head. Glorious sensations of the most indescribable feelings permeate me to the core and I know that I am truly loved.

I awoke from the vision in a state of bewilderment. The hand had demonstrated such incredible tenderness and gentleness and I knew instantly that I was more kind and loving because of its existence. My Divine Union, the essence of my Spirit had been physically linked to me, anchoring our love in this earthly world. A blinding headache accompanied deep times of cleansing. Like layers of an onion we peel away our imperfections one step at a time.

My fear of failure diminished with the experiences of my dream visions. I had no fear now as I walked with my heart hand in hand with the glory of this higher love.

Gathering Ties That Bind

The hint of a rainbow suddenly explodes with colours of vibrancy and vitality as it shimmers through teardrops of rain. Instead of finding pain in my heart, now I feel a deep connection toward the elements of nature. I feel the wind soar through my muscles, I feel the ocean slide through my veins, I feel the heat of fire combust in my heart and I feel the trembling of the earth in my bones. I am acutely aware of our connection to all that is. I am a storyteller.

My fear of failure and lack of confidence have been constant stumbling blocks. Now a higher source of love has created a path to truth. I have finally conceded that Divine Union is the key that links our differences as we learn to honour this truth. I was born to facilitate a process of healing that shows others a way to reach toward our true selves. The journey from fear to love is now upon us. It is our choice to choose this way of healing and freedom or to choose the way of ignorance through pain and suffering. Your own experiences offer the connection to obtain the key you seek. I can only guide you out of the cavern of darkness, showing you the way into the light.

In a few short years, I realise that my life as I know it today will change. It is my destiny to relay information through the process of writing. As I do so, I draw you into the recess of the truth of your being and for a time you are transported to a place of mystique, where you feel the tangible essence of truly knowing and loving yourself. It has been my intention to allow you a view into the journey of my life. You opened your heart while reading my story, quietly walking by my side. I feel as if I have always known you were there. I have felt you share my pain, cry with my tears, rejoice in my happiness of resolution and swoon in euphoria as I shared the intimacy of Divine Union. For my experiences are connected to yours and your experiences are connected to mine, for in truth, we are all one.

Looking for solutions that exist outside of us will not provide a permanent solution for the difficulties our world faces today. In the heart-wrenching depth of my pain, I did not have the strength or the foresight to see anything beyond my pain. It is only now that I have healed can I see a future that depicts a world where peace and abundance of life is a reality. For who we are is what we see. I am now able to accept a vision of cohesion and togetherness that we can all strive to obtain. As each person awakens to the glory of the real self through self-love, we take a permanent step toward our goals. Our outer world reflects our inner pain and suffering. As we heal our inner pain and suffering our outside world will heal and change. Know that you personally can and do make a difference. You are the difference.

Heaven on Earth and the information contained herein talks to you at the level of you. Its purpose is to enhance your own beliefs as there are many paths that lead us toward our ultimate destination. This information is dedicated to helping you journey with yourself so that you can find your truth through oneness.

The years gone by have produced many memorable glimpses of opening my heart as I share this euphoria with others. I have been given the opportunity to work with those who seek to follow the path of Divine

Union. The feeling of connection, of talking to one who knows the same pain and suffering is truly helpful. Be comforted by the knowledge that you do not journey through life alone.

I have conducted thousands of consultations for people regarding Divine Union. In doing so, I have discovered that so many people are awakening to their divinity themselves and searching for divine love. They speak of the glory of its being, they speak of their conventional marriages and relationships breaking down, they speak of frustration and anger, and they speak of hurt. Within the pain I see a glimmer of hope. Is there really a pure form of love we can experience that is our birthright? The answer is definitely yes. A light glistens in the depth of their eyes as I explain the phenomena of heart, body, soul and mind. A connection is made; the remembrance unlocks a door to the heart. The window of the soul awakens murmuring from its sleep to remember. They leave two hours later finer in heart and soul and with tools of resolution to begin their lives anew, confident to follow their life purpose and direction.

I view the work I do with reverent love and immense joy. My sense of humour and delight in the sublime has been my saving grace many times. During the past fifteen years I have met truly amazing people from varying backgrounds with life experiences and stories I love to hear. They have expanded my knowledge immensely and I express my heart-felt thanks and appreciation. One particular lady comes to mind, her name is Mary. She recently celebrated her ninety-eighth birthday.

Mary's husband Robert had passed away and she was feeling the intense loss of his loving presence in her life. They had shared sixty-six precious years together. Can you imagine my delight when Mary told me she knew all about Divine Union? She had lived it. As I watched this lady, tiny in stature, yet royal in heart and soul, I knew I was viewing a part of myself in the years that are yet to unfold.

Mary and Robert shared a love that exists within an infinite embrace. They are complements of one another, a perfect union of the original masculine and feminine essence of one Spirit. A beautiful photograph displays a snapshot of the couple in their late eighties holding hands. They experienced a need to touch, the light radiance and energy they felt when in each other's presence was tangible. They shared an amazing life together.

When I questioned Mary concerning her life and marriage with Robert she answered me with deep thought and reflection. She explained that loving each other is as easy as the breath we take in each moment. She also spoke of the purity of the depth of love they shared, of resolving their life issues quickly, and of allowing their love and trust to lead their lives forward. Mary and Robert located their Spirit through the subtle body which activates a merging of soul and spirit and the culmination of living their Higher Self on the earth. Their immense joy and happiness surrounded them, their families and all who found their way into their lives.

If you have chosen to do so, Divine Union will appear in your life in ways that are truly amazing. It will find you when you least expect it. Your heart will sing a song of sublime bliss and your feet won't seem to touch the ground.

Mary's friendship has been a tower of light, strength and resonance toward my understanding of Divine Union. She would often question her life purpose and wonder if she had achieved anything of significance. I would look at her in wonder and assure her that her life had been beneficial to many. Because of women like Mary we can access the wisdom of Divine Union first hand and the love that she and Robert experienced shines as a beacon of light so brightly that we may follow where they lead.

I have allowed Divine Union in the physical world and in my dream visions to lead me to wholeness and beyond. Wisdom affords us the opportunity to examine life and acknowledge challenge. Integrating knowledge into wisdom is a part of our human growth. These intense changes allowed this wisdom to filter through my heart and these words my soul knew.

I am not a victim of circumstances. I chose from my soul understanding the lessons I needed to learn this life. My biological parents Olivia and James gave me life. Their influence enabled me to foster a deep love of reading and my soul's love of music. My aunt Deanna provided a home for my spiritual connection and was my teacher of unconditional love. My former husband Antonio allowed us to finalise lifetimes of pain and suffering inflicted upon each other, to be healed and finally released. My children Luca, Marc, Bella and Lorenzo allowed me to practice true love. Andre allowed me the privilege to touch his heart while accessing the freedom to know the existence of Divine Union. Michael revealed that goodness resides in the heart of a man, the gift of friendship and the chance to accept and understand the value of healing. The Golden Man in my dream visions revealed the glory of my true essence, activated my life purpose and direction, demonstrated the subliminal love that accompanies the higher aspect of Divine Union and healed my fear in expressing this love. To my Divine Union, my future husband—now I am ready!

White Light of Love

Visioning imparts complexity in pure form. My experiences are woven into the tapestry of my being as I oscillate at this new level of awareness. Sensitivity is the founding form of expression as I become aware of a greater and deeper love for all that exists. New beginnings evolve into existence wrapped around the heart of patience, serenity and contentment. Father Time sits proudly watching the aura of our new birth.

My heart is ready, now open to receive the glory that awaits my life. In the form of a man, Divine Union will embrace my heart and soul and I smile at all there is yet to unfold. There is no need to rush toward filling my destiny. It unravels like strings of ribbon flying high in the flow of nature's sequential grace. Stillness sits in languid peace; silence speaks in hushed tones to the nature of my being. Shape and form ceases to exist in the embrace of purity. There is only the being of love.

We have come to the end of my story and yet, in truth, we have only just begun. New beginnings emerge from their cavern of quiet interlude. Am I scared? Am I frightened of the unknown equation that maps the unfolding of my future? The answer is no. I am more curious than nervous or scared for I know that only happiness and joy abounds.

A lifetime of experiences has emerged through my memories, the events having stood the test of time. It is only upon reflection that we realise the value of the wisdom we have obtained. It is the accumulated pain and suffering that disavows us the right to the purity of the truth of who we really are. The responsibility to awaken is ours. It is imperative to remember that when we feel anger, hurt, pain and intense frustration at those who have hurt us, it is only we who suffer. Resolution is the key required to step out of our limited emotional conditioning.

The cavern of the cocoon opens and a butterfly emerges. She sits perfectly still, her gossamer wings fluttering; her heart beats in unison with the evolving rotation of the earth. Her tiny body touches the ground, her heart soars through her wings in connection to all that is and she is alive with the glory of life. The purity of her grace is beautiful and I watch as she steadies herself preparing to fly to new horizons discovering the world that awaits her. She turns her miniature body toward me looking directly into my eyes before she takes flight. I notice her grace in stillness and peacefulness in silence as she shimmers with confidence and delight. A golden glow hovers around her tiny perfect form and I know that she exudes her essence in reflection of me.

My cocoon is peeled away and I now stand as the essence of the butterfly. I can almost feel the beauty of gossamer wings as golden light hovers around my shoulders and head. My emotional baggage has been accumulated and is now being boarded onto a train of no return. As I stand watching, the engine chugs softly as the train silently slides into oblivion. Quiet acceptance forms in the sense of knowing. The journey to release this baggage has been experienced upon a long and winding road.

There have been many times in my life where I have fallen. There have been many times when I have failed. There have been times when I have been stuck, unable to see my way clear. I know with absolute certainty that I have never walked this life path alone even though I have felt lonely and isolated many times. During the times of loneliness I know that it is me who has pushed this higher loving presence away for it cannot live in my emotional instability. It is my responsibility to move toward our higher source of love.

Divine Union is a gift. It is our birthright should we choose to acknowledge and accept it. Our world is constantly changing as we evolve in a new millennium. This time of transition has seen our world suffer through the effects of terrorism, inequality, wars raging in the name of God and the devastation of human lives lost to the ravages of nature's destruction. Through these times of tragedy we are brought together as the family of humanity. Why does the pain of tragedy bring us together? Why is this so? Why can't the gift of love bridge our gaps and provide a link that combines our differences? It can. If we allow divine love to let it do so.

One of the most important things I have discovered is this. If there is no love in your heart for yourself then you have no love to give another. You can only give what you have. Self-love, love to yourself through the acceptance of every part of you, is the first step forward. Acknowledge that you matter, that you are as sacred as the next person. We are all pure sparks of light living on earth evolving toward oneness. If you do this then you make a difference. If you choose to think this way then you are developing a greater sense of awareness and have stepped into the process of awakening, freeing your heart to access your Spirit.

During this time of our evolutionary growth we are experiencing a greater opportunity to heal the family. We are born to access a purity of love that links us in heart, body, soul and mind. There is no separation only blindness peeking through veils of illusion. The immense changes we will experience in our personal relationships will forever change the world as we know it. Divine Union is a love between two people that endures, it grows in strength and purity as it opens the portal to knowing and living our Higher Selves while living on earth. To live the purity of this love is the greatest gift we can know.

It is not my intention to advocate divorce on a whim. If you are experiencing love, joy and happiness in your relationship or marriage, then you are definitely on the right path. My intention is to offer support and encouragement to those who are seeking love again, to assist those to heal the rifts that have chained certain people to conventional relationships that have ended. To our youth—our future parents—I show you a way out of the maze of confusion and bad choices. To those who have endured a divorce or permanent separation these words I say from my heart. Be brave, heal your heart and let love in again, with purity this time not accumulated pain and suffering. We do not have to grow through fear, loss and desolation. Divine love is just one step away.

A Future Glimpse

A clear vision shimmers into view and I am woken in a dream vision. My conscious reality is stable as thoughts filter quietly through my mind. I find myself looking down at my body—the observer and the witness—as I sleep peacefully in my bed. Intrigue lingers. I am talking to a man dressed in a pure white robe, with long hair flowing down his back. Luminous eyes twinkle with wisdom and knowledge as he gently kneels before me. I am lying on my back with my hands crossed over my chest in deep repose. We should naturally assume that all is quiet when we sleep.

I know that he is a being of true knowledge and immense wisdom. He informs me that it is imperative I remember our conversation, stressing the importance of Divine Union's teachings. With the gentle command of authority while exuding pure love, he asks me if I understand. My heart resonates in quiet acknowledgement and I nod my head in agreement, affirming that his instruction is understood.

Another vision slowly shimmers into view. A doorway opens and I can see into a room filled with people. The atmosphere indicates a bubbly, up-beat energy as people are conversing with gusto. Animated expressions of delight skim the veneer of smiling faces. The intensity of Divine Union hits my heart with force and I breathe deeply. A man is approaching me from across the room. He is wearing a beautiful suit, a crisp white shirt and a blue tie. Before too long he is standing beside me, searching the depths of my eyes to connect to my true being. It is the complement of my heart and soul, it's my Divine Union. It is the essence of the beautiful man from my dream visions looking at me intently.

I am ecstatic that he really is alive in this world. I have to consciously remind myself to breathe and act naturally as I am not sure if he remembers for now who I am. I look into eyes that mirror my own. His love cascades in, through and around my heart. Time stands still allowing the touch of our inner divine hearts and lifetimes of memories flood my existence. Smiling at him, I remember his touch, the wonderment of soft, velvety kisses swirl within me. His eyes search mine and my heart skips a beat. My feet don't seem to touch the ground. There is immense relief that all I have seen in future visions will unfold in divine time. I watch transfixed as he leaves. We will meet again, this I know. The vision slowly shimmers and is gone.

The 1st of January 2006 dawns as a perfect summer day. I am woken in a dream vision as I feel intense pain in my lower abdomen. Looking down at my body, I see that I am pregnant and ready to give birth. My conscious reality panics. I have no memory of carrying this child. I look around and find that I am alone in my bedroom, lying on my ebony wrought-iron bed and not in a hospital with the support of doctors and nurses. Natural instinct takes over and I scream loudly for someone to assist me with the birth. All is still and quiet except for the sound of my heavy breathing as I labour through contractions. An overwhelming desire to push overpowers me.

There is no time to think or do anything except to allow Mother Nature to take action. For some inexplicable reason, I have to do this alone. The fullness of a head pushes its way through the birth canal as I remind myself not to panic. I have done this before and I can do it again. Four more pushes and the baby is born. Very carefully, I position my hands to catch the precious gift that has been bestowed on me when I realise there is no baby there. Opening my eyes, I see golden light hovering in a space in front of me. Swirling within *the light is a book. It is rotating around and around in a perfect circle. I am spellbound by the scene unfolding before me. The front cover depicts the words Heaven on Earth. I am overwhelmed by the feeling of grace. Tears of relief and wonderment trickle down my face. Each chapter is a story within itself, each lesson a labour of feelings to acknowledge, accept and heal. Heaven on Earth is born into the world.*

I awoke to the feeling of sheer delight. Golden sunbeams were beaming on the right hand side of the window reminding me that I am very much alive and well. My inner heart is now connected. Divine love's energy surges within me so familiar in truth. It is with honour and joy that I welcome Divine Union into my life once again allowing the optimal experience life has to offer.

I step once more into the frontier of heart, body, soul and mind. Take my hand and walk with me.

Now the awakening deepens and Heaven on Earth begins!